FAR BEYOND DEFENSIVE TACTICS

D1039374

This is the law:
The purpose of fighting is to win;
There is no possible victory in defense,
The sword is more important than the shield,
And skill is more important than either.
The final weapon is the brain.
All else is supplemental.

—John Steinbeck

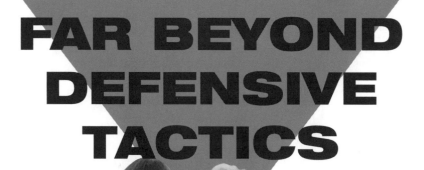

FAR BEYOND DEFENSIVE TACTICS

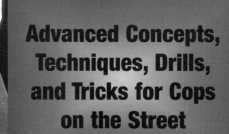

Advanced Concepts,
Techniques, Drills,
and Tricks for Cops
on the Street

Loren Christensen

PALADIN PRESS • BOULDER, COLORADO

Also by Loren Christensen:

Deadly Force Encounters
Fighting Power
Gangbangers
Restraint and Control Strategies (video)
Speed Training
The Way Alone

Far Beyond Defensive Training:
Advanced Concepts, Techniques, Drills, and Tricks
for Cops on the Street
by Loren Christensen

Copyright © 1998 by Loren Christensen

ISBN 0-87364-986-9
Printed in the United States of America

Published by Paladin Press, a division of
Paladin Enterprises, Inc.
Gunbarrel Tech Center
7077 Winchester Circle
Boulder, Colorado 80301 USA
+1.303.443.7250

Direct inquiries and/or orders to the above address.

Visit our Web site at www.paladin-press.com

Table of Contents

Preface

I have written this book with the full understanding and appreciation that both sexes are out there doing the job of policing and that both sexes are committing crimes. But for the ease of writing and reading, I use the male gender, he and him, when talking about cops and crooks.

I also recognize that law enforcement is made up of police officers, sheriffs' deputies, troopers, agents, marshals, security officers, and so on. To simplify, I use the word *officer* and pray that I don't offend anyone.

The use of physical force is called by many terms: *physical force confrontation, brawl, beef, use-of-force situation, goat rope, pig pile, ass thumpin'*, and other more colorful terms. To simplify, I have reduced these to one word: *fight*. Whether I am talking about a mild resist situation that requires a wristlock or a Wild West-style saloon brawl with flying chairs and thumping batons, I simply use the word *fight*.

Throughout the book I refer to other books I have written for Paladin Press. No, I am not seizing the moment to make shameless plugs (though way in the back of my mind, where things are dark and sinister, that may be part of the motivation). I do it to inform you of books where certain ideas are expanded upon. I don't mention all my books, and I even name some written by other authors. So, see?

I don't discuss handcuffing to any extent, other than when it relates to a specific principle or concept. I wanted to limit the subject of this book to the elements of fighting and the elements of avoiding a fight. Handcuffing is a complex subject and I would need another 200 pages to adequately cover it.

The fighting arts, of which defensive tactics is one, should never be complicated. Fighting is too fast, furious, and dangerous for complexity. If you find my approach to the subject simplistic, then I have accomplished my objective.

Introduction

When I began my career with the Portland Police Bureau in August 1972, I tried to keep it secret that I was a big, bad karate guy, but word got out and, while still on my 18-month probation as a new officer, I was promptly recruited into teaching defensive tactics to recruits hired not too long after me.

Although I was still soaking wet behind my ears, I nonetheless took on the task with great zeal and with absolutely no idea what the hell I was doing. I was a replacement for a judo-trained officer who for years had been teaching academy recruits a curriculum of falling drills, hip throws, and so-called come-along holds. While his teachings were marginally applicable to police work, the material I taught to my first four academies was even less applicable.

I thought I was passing on some very profound stuff. I was ignorant of grappling techniques, since my roots were in a karate style that emphasized tournament competition, which is to say, sport fighting. So it was sport-fighting techniques that I taught, drilling my recruits in karate punches, backfists, and a variety of kicks. I taught them traditional Japanese karate blocks and deep-rooted stances, making them do hundreds of them.

Learning defensive tactics was not a priority to the police department then, so the new recruits only received about eight hours of my wisdom, spread over three or four training sessions. When they completed their defensive tactics training, most of them could punch and kick as well as any average karate student with the same amount of time on the mat. The students liked what I taught them, but then they didn't have anything to compare it to. They thought they were getting some good stuff that would help them on the street, and so did I. But was the training applicable to what police officers needed? Not one bit.

It wasn't until two years and four academies later that I began to put together a program that fit the needs of working street officers. This new material didn't come to me in a dream, nor was I visited by a spirit warrior who mystically passed on the knowledge to me, two claims often cited by ancient Chinese and Japanese martial arts masters. I got my ideas from *Police Weaponless Control and Defense Techniques*, written by Robert Koga, a Los Angeles police officer, martial artist, and defensive tactics instructor. His approach made me do a 180-degree turn on how I thought about police defensive tactics, how I collected techniques, and how I taught them. There were lots of new ideas in that book, but there was one word Koga used over and over that made a huge impression on me: *control*.

Koga said that the sole objective in a physical force situation is to control the suspect. If you don't have control of him, you are vulnerable to whatever he wants to do to you, and you are at risk of either over- or underreacting when an arrest situation requires the use of greater force.

Well, that principle has been around for a long time now, and one can hope that most police agencies use it as a basic premise for their defensive tactics program. But in 1973 when I read Koga's book, the concept of control wasn't being used in many police agencies, including mine. I certainly didn't teach control to my first few academy classes; I taught those new officers to smash people with their fists, their feet, and a straight baton. I guess those are control techniques of a sort, since an unconscious suspect is no longer out of control. We got away with these "control techniques" back in the early 1970s, but they are unacceptable today because our society has evolved into one that demands that its police force be warm and fuzzy and do a lot of hugging.

Though my roots were in the punching and kicking arts, it dawned on me that having a goal of control actually made it easier to deal with a suspect who was resisting. I discovered that control gives you direction, a clear objective. Although kicking some dirtbag in the cookies (the cookies lie between the legs) might give you a wonderful sense of satisfaction, it also creates a lot of paperwork, the need for medical attention, and the potential for a lawsuit—and, this is the really important issue, it doesn't always control the guy.

I also discovered that when you keep the concept of control in the forefront of your mind, it helps you control yourself. Let's face it, sometimes you get pissed, and without a clear objective, there is an overpowering tendency to grab the jerk who pissed you off, dribble him around the room, bounce him off the walls, and then slam-dunk him in a trash can. Again, this might give you a moment of pleasure, but it will also cause you months of stress while you get investigated by your agency and the judicial system and sued by the jerk's shyster attorney. This is less likely to happen, however, when your clear objective is to get control of the suspect and the situation, handcuff him with control, and place him in your patrol car with control.

All this suddenly made sense to me in 1973, and I began to think about ways to implement the idea into our defensive tactics program. Around this time my agency sent me to the Federal Bureau of Investigation (FBI) training center in Quantico, Virginia, for a weeklong class in defensive tactics. Thirty officers attended the training from 30 major cities around the country, but only two of them had a solid program of defensive tactics that emphasized control—both were from California, and both had trained with Robert Koga.

The two officers held the rest of us, including the FBI instructors, spellbound as they taught us techniques and other moves they had adapted to Koga's concept of maintaining maximum control when dealing with a suspect. They showed us how to use pain to get that control and how to apply handcuffs while never relinquishing control. Everything we did that week was about control.

I returned to Portland bubbling with new ideas to make our program a better one. I introduced the techniques and concepts at my next recruit academy, and within a few months our defensive tactics program took on a new look and a new validity. I no longer taught recruits to kick people in the cookies and smash noses with their fists. Now we practiced joint locks, leverage takedowns, and an assortment of other painful compliance techniques, things that officers could really use on the job.

Since those early years, our program has expanded from one instructor (little ol' me) to a cadre of more than 30. I stepped down as lead instructor in 1980, because of demands on my time from other duties in the bureau, to the less time-consuming position of number two. In the mid-1980s, I was transferred to the Gang Enforcement Team where my time was even more limited, which forced me to restrict my teaching to in-service training only.

Portland's program has expanded and improved over the years. New recruits now get more hours of defensive tactics training than ever before, and uniformed officers in the precincts get monthly refresher training and even more training in the annual week-long, in-service training.

Many of the ideas I discuss in this book are a result of teaching defensive tactics to countless organizations outside the Portland Police Bureau. I have taught employees of various police agencies, colleges, mental health facilities, private security companies, and other organizations that need police-related techniques. I like teaching to outside agencies because I can introduce material that time constraints and political restrictions in Portland's agency don't allow for.

I began training in karate in 1965, and I still teach the arts of karate, jujitsu, and arnis in my private school. My students consist of uniformed police officers, detectives, and citizens interested in learning real self-defense, not sport fighting. As a guy with 29 years of experience in law enforcement and who has taught martial arts since 1965, I firmly believe that the Portland Police Bureau's defensive tactics program is one of the best in the country. Although it's still restricted by some problems discussed in this book, the program is nonetheless innovative, logical, and, what is most important, applicable to what the officers who are out there facing the dragon every day need.

This book is not about Portland's defensive tactics program, although some ideas discussed within are similar to or some variation of what it teaches. I can't avoid sharing those things with you because they work and prove themselves every day out on the mean streets. Portland's formal, documented program is copyrighted, which makes it a no-no for me to share it with you. However, I do discuss some of its techniques, concepts, and principles, which are universal and cannot be copyrighted, because they apply to certain facets of combat discussed in this book. Since I don't have to answer to a police administration, those men and women who don't know a wristlock from a banana, I have added subtle Christensen variations to make the techniques, principles, and concepts even better (sometimes it's hard to be humble).

I also take it upon myself to discuss lots of things I see wrong with defensive tactics programs around the country, as well as many things that I see right. I also talk about elements of defensive tactics that, because of budget limitations, time constraints, or management ignorance, I could never teach in Portland. These include physical training drills, mental exercises, philosophical approaches to fighting, and the importance of survival techniques when the poop hits the fan.

By the time you read this, I will have retired from the Portland Police Bureau. This allows me to do two things. First, I can go YIPPEE! Secondly, it allows me to say any damn thing I want about police management, city government, and bleeding heart citizens, three forces that are often a real thorn in the paw of police officers trying to do what needs to be done.

Police work is a crazy job, and it ain't getting any saner. Citizens want more from their police agencies now than ever before, yet they are quick to damn the police for the slightest infraction or perceived infraction. Sometimes it seems that citizens don't care about your risking your life as long as the rights of some low-life, scum-eating maggot are not violated, and this isn't going to change tomorrow or even next year. In fact, it will probably get worse. We are in a fuzzy-warm era now in policing and, if you have 20 years left before you retire, you just have to ride it out and hope that the next era is one that puts the rights of law-abiding citizens over those of the criminal element.

I hope that you have developed the philosophy that there isn't anything that is going to keep you from going home at the end of your shift. You owe it to yourself, your family, and your peers to be the best trained officer you can be. Your skill in defensive tactics is one very important aspect of your knowledge.

I hope this book gets you thinking about it.

Chapter 1

The Right Demeanor

With the proper demeanor, you can handle 99 percent of your person contacts without incident. So why are there some officers who have so many problems? You know who I am talking about, the ones who always call for backup because they have "a possible fighter" or they are already fighting with someone. Could it be the part of town they are working in or the shift? Sure. Nonetheless, there are always those officers who would get into three fights a week even if they were walking a foot beat in a convent.

I'll bet you a cup of coffee (or a latte, if you're that type of person) that the reason some officers get into so many fights is because of their negative demeanor. One officer has a chip on his shoulder, another is loud and abrasive, one is a badge-heavy bully, another is a know-it-all, and so on. These guys could piss off a bishop.

The correct demeanor is hard to describe. Some new officers have it naturally, and many veteran officers have it as a result of years of trial and error.

Look at old news reels of General Patton, or equally as good, watch George C. Scott play him in the movie, *Patton*. While one Patton had the right demeanor for real, and the other had it for the reel, both "Pattons" revealed a presence that shouted, "I'm in charge."

I belong to an organization called the American Teacher's Association of Martial Artists (ATAMA), an international organization of teachers from all styles of the fighting arts. The first time I attended one of its seminars in San Francisco, I was told not to be deceived by the head of ATAMA, a 10th-degree black belt named Duke Moore. Professor Moore earned his first black belt in 1940, and today his exploits and accomplishments in the martial arts are legendary.

The day of the seminar, as I was changing into my karate uniform, I noticed a little man in his late 60s walk slowly by. I didn't pay him any attention other than to have a passing thought that he must be the janitor. Wrong.

He removed his suit jacket and his fedora hat, then pulled a white judo uniform out of his bag. He slipped out of his street clothes, put on his uniform, and then reached into his bag and pulled out a red belt—Professor Moore is one of a few American 10th-degree black belts whose rank is recognized in Japan—and wrapped the belt around his waist and secured it as he had been doing for more than 50 years.

What impressed me more than the red belt and all that it symbolized was how Professor Moore's demeanor changed as he slipped out of his street clothes and into his warrior uniform. He converted from an "average senior citizen" to a leader with an unquestionable command presence. Later in the gym, when he stepped in front of 150 martial artists, most of whom were black belts, there was no question who was in charge: he was the master, the father; we were the students, the children. He was like General Patton in front of a company of privates. He never purposely dominated us with his demeanor; it was just there.

The professor was approachable, warm, and friendly, while maintaining an air of confidence that made us feel comfortable in his presence.

PRESENCE

New officers often display a demeanor that is of one extreme or the other: either timid or badge heavy. Either one can get an officer hurt. A streetwise punk will easily detect an officer's timidity and take advantage of it in a second. On the other hand, the officer who comes on too strong because he is overcompensating for his lack of confidence will often instigate a fight where one need not have happened.

On my second day on the job, my coach and I were arresting a verbally nasty motorist for driving under the influence. I was trying my best to appear like I had been on the job for years, acting with what I thought was a salty swagger, a menacing frown, and a tough way of talking out of the corner of my mouth. Just when I was convinced that our prisoner was convinced, he asked me, "You new, ain't yuh, kid?" You could hear the wind rush out of my sails.

Understanding your job and knowing that you can handle most situations, physical and otherwise, will show itself through that intangible quality called aura. It can be felt by others as it communicates to them that you know what you are doing and that you have command of the situation. Or, as a friend of mine, who is a kickboxer and a police officer, says, "Assholes know not to fuck with me because I will kill them." While that may be a little strong and not in line with today's warm and fuzzy approach to police work known as community policing, this officer has definitely established a demeanor that works for him.

Here are a few components that make up a positive, strong demeanor:

- Good posture (your mother was right)
- Eye contact
- A clean, pressed uniform

- Physical fitness
- Strong hand gestures (keep them out of your pockets)
- Knowledge of the job
- A take-charge attitude (though not "in your face" pushy)

VOICE

Although using your voice properly is part of your demeanor, I am separating them here for ease of discussion. Your voice must leave no doubt that you are in control and that it's your ball game. You got called to the family fight because the participants were unable to settle the situation themselves. They needed, or maybe it was the neighbors who felt they needed, a third party to intercede. You got the call and left whatever you were busy doing to go restore peace. Now you are at the scene, and, whether the combatants like it or not, you are in charge. If you aren't, they are going to run right over you.

Generally, your presence at a call will be noticed first, followed by your voice. A weak, woosie voice is not going to control anything or anyone. It needs to be strong, clear, and authoritative, projecting to all that the police are here, and the police are in charge. As with your physical demeanor, your voice needs to be authoritative without being badge heavy or overbearing.

This is a fine line, and it takes a while for some officers to find it. Listen to yourself and be aware of the reactions you get from people, or ask your fellow officers how you sound. Make an effort because you can accomplish much with the right tone of voice.

A good, strong voice has the following qualities:

- Proper volume
- Crisp, clear diction
- Articulate enunciation

Improper use of the voice has these traits:

- Challenging tone

- Pleading tone
- Bullying tone
- Argumentative tone

There is no arguing that a professional demeanor and a strong, authoritative voice will go a long way toward keeping you out of fights. Some officers come by them naturally; some learn them through trial and error. Be aware of how you come across to people and emulate those who have already found it. Realize that a big part of proper demeanor and voice comes from confidence in knowing your profession and knowing how to take care of yourself physically.

ASK, TELL, MAKE

Here is a technique that works more times than not. I used it for years because it usually worked for me. I don't remember if I came up with it on my own, or if I stole it from one of the old, salty veteran beat cops I was blessed to work around when I first put on the uniform. Wherever I got it, I am grateful.

Until now, I never gave it much thought as a formal procedure. Coincidentally, however, while working on this book that you so wisely bought, I came across an article entitled "Ask * Tell * Make: Street Negotiations Made Easy" in the March 1997 issue of *The Police Marksman* magazine. In it, author David R. Kidder brilliantly structured the technique so that it's easy to understand and practical to use.

The technique is based on the assumption that you want to control every situation you are in without the use of force—that is, you want every person to voluntarily comply with your requests. Though you are the toughest officer in your agency, control is a whole hell of a lot easier when you can get people to cooperate with you. I know, I know, there are some dirtbag scumbuckets you want to thump with a whole lot of street justice. The problem is that while that may reward you with momentary satisfaction, there is just too much inherent risk involved in today's climate to give people what they deserve. You risk injury to yourself, injury to the suspect, and a lawsuit. I have experienced all three of these, so let this aging scrapper tell you that it's far better to get cooperation. It's this premise that I am going to proceed with here.

Here is how it works. First, you ask a person to do something. Second, if asking fails, you tell him to do it. Finally, you make him do it if telling him fails. I don't have any percentages to give you, but from my experience, I've found that asking works most of the time when you do it correctly. Don't think like officers who believe that asking shows weakness and that a police officer should never have to ask for compliance. This is nonsense.

When you ask someone to do something, using a professional demeanor and with an attitude that conveys the message that what you are asking for will be done, you will come across as possessing power and authority. In addition, by asking properly, you will be perceived as respectful, a trait that often gets returned in kind. Respect begets respect.

What have you got to lose by asking? Nothing. If the person complies, you have been successful. If he doesn't comply, then you advance to the next step, which is to tell him what to do. You are not out anything, and, in fact, you have actually gathered a small piece of intelligence about the suspect. Also, it looks good in your report when you ask first, because you can write that you asked for cooperation, but the suspect refused. So you had no choice but to take the next step up the ladder.

Let's say you come upon two men arguing on the sidewalk. You decide to talk to the one with the bloody nose first. You ask the other guy, "Sir, would you please step over there by my car? I'll hear your side in a minute." But he doesn't move and continues to shout and threaten the guy with the bad nose. The stage has been set for you to advance up a rung and tell the man what you want him to do.

There are two levels of telling that you can try. An example of low-level telling would be to tell the guy who refuses to step aside momentarily, "I need you to step over by my car until I am ready to talk to you." High-level telling would sound like this,

"Get over by my car. Now!" Most people will obey your order in one or the other of these levels. For those who don't obey, you must advance a rung on the ladder and make them. You are justified in making them do what you want because you first asked them and then told them, but they refused to comply with both of these low-level approaches.

It's the person's refusal to cooperate that escalates the situation to one where you have to use force. How much force depends on the situation. A simple wristlock might do the trick or maybe a 9mm round, or perhaps it might take running over the guy with your police car. The situation dictates the type of force needed to elicit cooperation.

Of course, you don't always have to go in the order of ask, tell, and make. For example, if you were to walk around the corner and find a gun barrel pointing straight at your nose, you are not going to respond, "Good evening, sir. Would you mind laying down that .45 caliber semiauto?" Instead, you would duck, bob, weave, backpedal, fill your shorts, and pump a mag of rounds into the gunman's body.

But even if you need to jump right into a "make" situation, telling the suspect what you want him to do can still be helpful. Let's say the guy waiting for you around the corner has a stick instead of a .45, and he has it cocked over his shoulder in preparation to smack you with it. You choose to respond with your baton. You lunge in with a strike to his elbow, and tell him repeatedly, "Get down! Get down, now!" Though he winces from your blow, he continues to advance toward you. Again you hit him, this time against his shins, again telling him loudly, "Get down, now!" He obeys, partly because of the pain you have inflicted on him and partly because of your strong commands that gave him direction.

By the way, keep in mind that not every pain technique gives direction. While the pain caused by some joint lock techniques is unquestionably clear about which direction the suspect should go, other techniques hurt without giving direction. Slamming a baton into someone's elbow and knee does not give clear direction, though it hurts like hell. Pain combined with clear commands should erase any doubt in the suspect's mind about what you want him to do.

As discussed in Chapter 6, "How to Create a Witness," when you verbalize your demands loudly and clearly as you wrestle, strike with your baton, or blaze away with your weapon, you create witnesses from those people watching. When they see you fight with a combative suspect, all their experiences and prejudices about the police, good or bad, color what they see. When you repeatedly tell the suspect what to do, it will help color in the minds of the witnesses what they are seeing.

"Ask * Tell * Make" is designed to reduce your chance of having to use force. Sure, you may enjoy a good fight occasionally, but there is always an inherent risk, and that risk far outweighs the fun.

Chapter

2

Techniques, Principles, and Concepts

In the business of fighting—whether it's offensive, defensive, or for purposes of simple control—there exist techniques, principles, and concepts. It's not uncommon to hear martial artists and police officers use these words interchangeably, though this is grossly inaccurate. It's true that they all have to do with fighting and are all interrelated somewhat, but they are still separate. Allow me to clarify.

TECHNIQUES

Fighting techniques are the wristlocks, takedowns, baton strikes, punches, kicks, pinches, eye gouges, throat stomps, and groin smashes used to gain control of, or to defend against, suspects who choose to resist you. There are lots of techniques in existence, thousands and thousands, but not all are applicable to the specific needs of law enforcement. In fact, most are not. There are basically four categories of techniques used in law enforcement:

1. Techniques for control
2. Techniques for defense
3. Techniques for offense
4. Techniques for survival

Techniques for Control
These are used most often in police work since the objective of every situation is to get control. Control is gained through some of the following techniques:

- The officer's presence
- The officer's demeanor
- The officer's voice
- The officer's body position
- The officer "asking" or "telling" a person to do something
- The officer "making" a person do something by using:
  Physical control
  Impact weapons
  Deadly force

Techniques for Defense
These are techniques used to defend against an assailant's attack.

- Blocking
- Dodging
- Evading

Techniques for Offense
Offensive techniques are used to attack a suspect, such as the following:

- Punching, kicking
- Striking with a baton
- Grabbing
- Pulling, pushing, shoving, tripping
- Using a chemical spray
- Shooting
- Manipulating joints
- Applying pressure against nerve points

Techniques for Survival

It's anything goes when fighting to survive. The following are some common survival techniques:

- Shooting
- Stabbing
- Punching
- Kicking
- Hitting with a brick
- Running over an assailant with a vehicle

All of the above techniques work best when they are applied in conjunction with principles and concepts.

PRINCIPLES

Techniques change, but principles are constant. For example, the principle of gravity states that what goes up must come down, at least here on Earth. If you toss an apple into the air, gravity pulls it back down. But you can use a variety of techniques to throw the apple up: overhand, underhand, through your legs, or under your armpit. No matter what technique you use to throw it, the principle of gravity pulls the apple back.

Understanding the principles that relate to fighting is important, because without an understanding of them, you are a floundering ship at sea, simply moving around, relying on luck to get you through the storm. There are only a few physical principles in existence, and they are easy to understand.

Keep in mind techniques can change, but not the laws to which they apply.

Control

Control is often considered a concept, but for law enforcement purposes, I think of it as a principle, an unchanging law. If you don't have control of a situation and of the people in it, you ain't got nothin'. Your primary objective, whether you are at an armed robbery, a domestic fight, or a tavern brawl, is to get control fast. When you are face-to-face with a suspect, it's imperative that you establish control quickly, because if you don't, he remains dangerous.

Control is established through your presence, your voice, your body position, your control holds, your baton, your chemical spray, and your gun. You must get control quickly and by whatever means necessary.

As discussed earlier, by having control as an objective in every situation and in every person contact, you will have greater control over yourself. You are less likely to flail away madly in a fight when you have a clear goal of maneuvering the suspect into a position to be handcuffed, rather than fighting until he has been beaten into the soil. The more in control you are over yourself—because of your clear objective—the less chance there is of your overreacting and getting slapped with a charge of using excessive force.

Action/Reaction

Action is faster than reaction, or, to put it another way, reaction is slower than action. If you are standing within striking range of a motorist as you write a citation, it will be almost impossible for you to defend against his surprise attack. He first has to make a decision to punch you in the chops and then his brain has to send a message to his muscles to launch his big hairy knuckles at your nose. He makes this decision and puts it into action while you are oblivious and happily writing his ticket. When you do see his action, your eyes must send an alarm to your brain where it bounces around to four specific locations before it sends a message to your muscles to raise your arm and try to block the attack. But because you are so close to him and his action is already set into motion, your reaction takes too long and your arm rises too late. You eat his fist.

A simple technique to apply to the action/reaction principle is to stand a little greater than arm's reach from everyone you talk with. This distance is called "the gap," and it not only creates space, but also time for you to react. Although the motorist can still pop a punch at you, he has to close the gap, which provides you with a little extra time to react to his action. And when you are trained and mentally prepared, that's all you need—just a little more time.

Knowledge of the action/reaction principle is important when someone has you at gunpoint. In this scary situation, you are going to initiate the action, which means the suspect has to react to you. Now, if he is pointing the gun at you from 10 feet away, the only action you are going to initiate is to fill your pants. You have to use all your bullshit ability to get to a range where you can touch his weapon. Try showing pictures of your kids or promising him a new car. Say whatever it takes to get close. Only when you are within touching range should you ever attempt to disarm him and only then when you are absolutely convinced you are going to be shot.

As we discuss in Chapter 5 ("Do Whatever It Takes to Survive"), to increase the gunman's reaction time to your movement, you should talk to him, or better yet, get him to talk. When his brain is busy listening to your words or busy formulating his own words, he has to change mental gears suddenly when you make a move for his gun. For sure, he can do this quickly, but if you are physically trained and mentally geared to move, you can swat his gun aside before he can shoot you. If he pulls the trigger at all, his shot will go off into space.

The action/reaction principle works even when the gunman has his arm wrapped around your neck and his gun screwed into your ear. I first learned this in an officer survival school in California several years ago and was amazed at how well it worked. In fact, it never failed, even when my training partner was anticipating what I was going to do. As soon as he had me in his hold and I felt the cold barrel against the side of my head, I would say something, like, "Are you ready?" I would either swat the gun back into his face as I asked the question, or I would swat it as he replied, "Yes." Either way, that hammer always dropped as the gun barrel was swatted away from my precious head and into his face.

Look at your training and think about other situations where the action/reaction principle can be applied.

Distraction

One time my partner and I chased an armed suspect across a yard, up onto his porch where several people were standing and sitting, and into his house. But when we caught him in his living room and patted him down, he no longer had the .38 revolver. A small child told us that his grandma out on the front porch had the gun. We learned later that as the suspect ran into the house, he dropped the gun into the big front pocket of the old blind woman's apron.

When we got to her, the 75-year-old blind woman had the gun in her hand, her finger in the trigger guard, and was waving it around in total confusion about what was happening. No one on the porch was telling her what was going on because they were too busy scrambling for their lives. My partner quickly grabbed her gun hand, but she held fast out of confusion from all the commotion that she was hearing. He pried desperately at her finger, but the harder he tried the more she stiffened her hand and finger.

I pushed our handcuffed prisoner against the wall with one hand and grabbed the old woman's index finger on her free hand with my other. As my partner pried at her trigger finger, which in her panic and confusion had become as strong as Arnold Schwarzenegger's, I bent back her other finger and said softly several times, "Let go of the gun, ma'am; we are the police." After a long moment, she yelped from the pain in her finger, and my partner took advantage of her distraction to pull her other finger away from the trigger.

Whenever my partner and I reminisce about this, we refer to it as the time we beat up the old blind woman.

An officer squeezes a suspect's neck cord to cause enough pain to distract the suspect's thoughts from gripping the steering wheel.

The distraction principle states that a person can only think of one thing at a time. Remembering this will go a long way toward helping you not look foolish as you struggle to bend a suspect's stiffened arm, pry loose an enraged wife's hand from her husband's hair, or pull a suspect's arms out from under his prone body.

Let's say you have decided to take a motorist into custody, but he white-knuckles his steering wheel and refuses to get out. You reach in and try to remove his hand, but he has a death grip that a crowbar couldn't pry loose. His entire thought process is on his grip, and the harder you try to release it, the harder he squeezes. His concentration, his entire being, is focused on not letting you pry his hand free. To win this struggle, you must change the course of his thinking.

Reach up with your other hand and squeeze a cord in his neck, twist a few of the short hairs on the back of his head, or flick your finger against the corner of his eye. These techniques will cause acute pain and sometimes a startle reflex. In either case, the suspect's attention and his entire thinking process are briefly distracted from his hand. It's at this exact moment that you pry his hand free of the steering wheel.

Let's say when you grab a suspect's arm to apply a wristlock, he stiffens it. Even a child who stiffens her arm can be a challenge to a big, burly police officer like you. This is where distraction helps you to not look foolish or like a big bully. To distract his concentration from his arm, pinch the soft, tender skin inside that upper arm, jab your thumb into his tender rib area, or ram your knee into the peroneal nerve at the side of his thigh. These and other sharply delivered techniques will momentarily distract him from his frozen arm and provide you with a window of opportunity to bend the hell out of it.

The nice thing about distraction techniques is that they can be subtle, yet still effective. The suspect's friends won't know that you just gave their buddy a shock of pain, though they will wonder why he suddenly began cooperating with you.

Yielding

The principle of yielding, sometimes called "going with the flow," is basic to most grappling arts. It's what helps a small person defeat a larger person, a weaker person to defeat a stronger person.

Let's say you are holding a guy with one hand on his upper arm and your other on his wrist. As you start to escort him to your police car, he lunges to ram his shoulder into you. However, since you wisely bought this book and understand the principle of yielding, you are not going to resist his assault, but rather yield to it. Maintain your grip on his arm as you sidestep, allowing his energy to flow past you. You then whip his arm into a control hold or add your energy to his and drive him face-first into a wall (I've always liked that choice).

When you have developed skill at yielding, it means you don't have to worry any more about the other guy's size. Well, that might be overstating it a little since you always have to consider the other guy's size, especially when he is 12 inches

The officer is walking a suspect when the suspect suddenly thrusts his shoulder toward the officer. The officer yields to the suspect's force by grabbing his neck and spinning him around and ka-thunk! *slamming him into a wall.*

The officer is in a clinch with the suspect, who is starting to win. The officer kicks the suspect in the ankle to divert his attention downward and then executes a clothesline technique up high.

taller and 150 pounds heavier than you. However, when you have the skill to yield to his force, as opposed to trying to stop him with your inferior force, you greatly increase your chance of being successful.

My youngest daughter was 5 years old when she began training in the martial arts, and by the time she was 6 she could block my biggest student's straight punch. This is because she didn't attempt to stop the force, but instead leaned slightly away as she parried it a few inches off its course. To say it another way, she didn't pit her relatively weak force against the big puncher's, but simply used what force she did possess to move the superior one aside.

A beneficial and fun way to understand the concept of yielding is to take hold of your partner's upper arms or shoulders as he takes hold of yours and then move around the mat together. When he jerks on one of your arms to pull you, don't resist, but go with his pull. When it's your turn to push him, he should respond by pulling you toward him, or sidestepping your force and pulling you by. Although there may be occasions when resisting is your best option, most often, yielding to the pull or push will be the easiest path to take.

After you yield to your partner's force, your goal is to apply a control hold or take him to the floor. Remember, yielding is just half the battle; you still need to get control of him so you can apply handcuffs. Start simply. Hold on to your partner's upper arm and wrist as he slowly nudges your shoulder and then sidestep and maneuver his arm into the most applicable hold. Repeat this until you can do it smoothly. Develop skill and confidence at a slow pace before you ever attempt to do it hard and fast.

Yielding often works well with transitioning (see Chapter 4). When you attempt one technique and meet resistance, flow with that resistance and let it take you into another technique. This takes practice and an understanding of your techniques, but then that's what I harp on all the way through this book. Knowledge is power.

High/Low

This is a frequently used principle in my karate classes, and it's also applicable in police work, though it's seldom used or taught.

In karate, it's used as an offensive technique to direct our opponent's mind where we want it to go. For example, to get an opponent's attention to a low target on his body, the attacker will kick his knee or shin, distracting the opponent long enough to strike him in the face. The opponent will usually think, *My leg!* whether the attacker actually hit him there or only faked a kick. If he were indeed struck in the lower leg, his thought process will be on the blow, especially if it hurts. If the kick is just a low fake, the opponent will be thinking about not getting hit. Whether the kick makes contact or is only a fake, it will take a moment for the opponent to switch his mental gears (this is where the distraction and action/reaction principles overlap), which gives the attacker a moment to deliver an attack to the opponent's head.

Depending on what the situation calls for, the karate fighter can also hit or fake to a high target first and then follow with a low blow. If the karate fighter wants to psychologically screw with his opponent even more, he could hit him low, then high, then low, then high again. I have found that with most opponents—and with myself when it has been done to me—the brain shuts down, or gives up, after three or four rapid-fire high/low hits. When this happens, the attacker can pretty much do whatever he wants to his opponent.

The high/low principle works well with the police baton. Whip the baton across the guy's knee and then back across his elbow, or lead with a high blow to his upper arm and then bring the baton down and across his shin or ankle. If the guy is especially ornery, smack him a third time to a high target, such as his elbow, and then whip the baton back down across his knee. After four high/low blows, his mind should be defeated, providing you with a window of opportunity to dump him on his butt for handcuffing.

You can also use the high/low principle to take a suspect to the ground using your empty hands. Say you have grabbed his arm to apply handcuffs, and he begins to vigorously twist his arm away from you. Since his thought is on his arm, a relatively high point on his body, kick his ankle bone with the toe of your shoe to distract his brain downward and then fling your arm across his upper chest and take him down backwards to the ground.

An alternate technique would be to swing his arm up high,

which also diverts his brain up high, then sweep his closest foot out from under him.

The high/low principle works well. Try it, you'll like it.

CONCEPTS

I was called in by Internal Affairs once to testify as an expert witness in an excessive force case involving one of our own officers. My department was trying to hang him for grabbing a suspect by the front of his shirt and jamming him into a wall, which tore the suspect's shirt and popped off some buttons. The department was siding with the suspect, saying that the officer's force and technique were inappropriate. If I had known I was being called in to testify against another officer, I would have called in sick or come up with some reason I couldn't do it. But I was stuck once I was in the door. So I had to be clever.

I was acquainted with the veteran officer in question, but I couldn't remember seeing him in any of my defensive tactics classes. A look through his file showed that he had somehow slipped through the cracks and had not received any training since I had changed the basis of our defensive tactics program to that of control. This oversight wasn't the officer's fault; it was the department's.

The investigators tried to get me to say that the officer's force and choice of technique were wrong. They were sort of right, but I wasn't going to admit that. I told them that grabbing someone by the shirt and pushing him into a wall was not a technique that I taught, but then the officer didn't know any of the techniques I taught because he had not been sent to the updated training. In spite of this, he knew he had to control the suspect, so he used the only technique he knew. His crude method worked, and he was able to get the suspect handcuffed.

Thanks to little ol' me, Internal Affairs begrudgingly threw the case out, and the officer went back to work a happy camper. I, however, had to dodge Internal Affairs for the next several months.

For our purposes, I define a concept as a thought process or an understanding that gives guidance in a defensive tactics situation. Concepts are ideas that, when adopted as your way of doing the job, increase your success rate and help keep you from being accused of wrongdoing.

Continuum of Control

There are many variations of this, but they all share similarities. Although it's good to believe that a continuum of control is going to provide you with guidance, the reality is that in a threatening situation on the street, you are going to be trying your best not to get sucker-punched, or worse. When a suspect comes at you with a hammer, you are not going to pause and reflect on where his actions fall in the continuum of control. You are going to be too busy backing up, spraying pepper, firing your weapon, or running like hell to be thinking about a little chart.

However, the continuum does act as a teaching aid and a guide to new and veteran officers about the expectations of the law, their agency, and the people they serve. It also educates the public about the use of force, and it's an informative tool in court to help a jury understand how officers deal with various levels of resistance. The following is one such chart.

Subject's Behavior	Control Level	Response Options
Cooperation	Mere presence	Officer's presence
Threatening demeanor	Verbal skill	Ask; tell
Mild resistance	Low-level physical control	Control holds
Greater than mild resistance	Intermediate physical control	Control holds, spray, baton
Aggressive, assaultive	Impact weapons	Baton, body weapons, spray
Serious assault, deadly force	Impact weapons, deadly force	Baton, firearm

Of course, you can go out of order depending on the situation. If the suspect is cooperative, you would start at the cooperation level, which is the lowest. But if he suddenly pulled a knife, you would jump all the way to the highest level, that of deadly force. That seems obvious, but there is always someone who asks if it's permissible. Sheesh!

The control continuum is a guide, a concept to keep in your mind and to articulate when explaining your actions in a report.

Police Work Is Not Competitive

"Oh sure, it took four of you stinking cops to get me cuffed. One of you couldn't do it. What a bunch of pussies."

I couldn't begin to count how many times I've heard a suspect say something like this after several officers wrestled him into handcuffs and into the backseat of a police car. Don't let these words tweak your machismo. Police work is not a contest, though many crooks (and not just a few police officers) are under the impression that it is. If you try to make it one, you dramatically increase the danger level of a job that is already dangerous. Police work is not sport—it is not a volleyball game or collegiate wrestling. There is no swatting each other on the rears like they do in the NFL, and there is no high-fiving (although I have seen officers embarrass themselves by doing high-fives on the TV show *COPS*).

Police work is a job, a weird and crazy one for sure, but nonetheless it's still just a job. Your objective in every contact with the citizenry, with every arrest and every physical confrontation, is to use every legal means at your disposal to achieve and maintain control.

A physical arrest has one clear objective: take the suspect into custody, chain him up, and put his butt behind bars. There is no place in this process for sport. If you make the arrest by yourself, fine (though it's always better to have backup). If it takes five officers to take one person into custody, that's fine too.

Have you ever heard this challenge from a suspect: "Hey, cop. Just you and me. I'm gonna kick your ass"?

Here is what I tell these jerks: "Well, maybe you can kick my ass. But then you're going to have to kick my partner's ass. And if you do that, he's going to call for another cop, and you're going to have to kick his ass, and then the next officer's ass, and the next. There are a thousand of us working tonight, and eventually you're going to get tired. Then we're going to kick your ass, and we're going to have fun doing it. Cause this ain't no contest, pal."

This works every time.

Police Officers Should Never Provoke a Fight

This can really test your self-discipline. When you snap the handcuffs on a slimy, greasy-haired, tattoo-covered, rotten-toothed piece of human waste who just raped a 1-year-old child and then repeatedly stuck her with the burning end of a cigarette, it can be tormentingly difficult not to handcuff the guy to your car bumper and take him for a high-speed ride over the humps at a drive-in theater.

I arrested a guy several times whose picture was in the dictionary next to the word *asshole*. One time, when I removed his handcuffs and chucked him into a holding cell, he spat at me, kicked at me through the bars, and swore he would kill my entire family. "Take off that gun," he screamed, "and I'll beat the shit out of you. You ain't nothin' without that gun."

I hated the maggot, and I was tired of having to fight every time I arrested him. I also had a headache, and I was in a cranky mood. So I jerked my gun out of its holster and put it into a gun locker and advanced toward him, with the sole objective of making his head lonesome for his shoulders.

"OK, OK, OK," he said quickly, sounding a lot like Joe Pesci in the *Lethal Weapon* movies. "If you didn't have that, uh, gunbelt on, I'd kick your ass."

So I unsnapped my rig and tossed it aside. I again moved toward him with happy thoughts of making his face a crimson mess. "OK, OK, OK," he said. "If you didn't have that, uh, blue shirt and that badge on, I'd kick the shit out of you."

"Not a problem," I said and began unbuttoning my shirt.

"You know," my partner said, who had been leaning against a cell and watching the show with a bemused look on his face. "You're just provoking the guy, and he's provoking you. Pretty soon he's going to have you down to your skivvies, and, let's face it, you don't got that good of legs."

That was enough to snap me back to reality. I shut the cell door and got my gear back on, and my partner and I went back to the street. I arrested the creep a couple more times over the next few months, but managed to keep my temper—and my clothes on.

Your job is not to provoke, but to maintain a professional distance. You are to enforce the laws, not force people into breaking them—such as trying to get them to take a swing at you—so you can then do a tap dance on their face while you arrest them. Yes, at times this can be one of the most difficult challenges of the job, but you must do it for the sake of law enforcement and for the sake of keeping your job.

The suspect raises his fists. The officer doesn't try to compete against him with the same force, but instead draws his baton in order to dominate the situtation.

Dominate the Situation

"You don't take a knife to a gunfight," goes the old saying. I define this as meaning you take to your task whatever is necessary to get the job done safely for you and your fellow officers. If there is one suspect, take two or more officers. If he raises his fists, hit him with your baton. If he pulls a knife, shoot him with your gun. If he uses a pistol, you use a shotgun.

You must approach every situation with the mind-set that you are in charge, that you will be the dominant figure and the dominant force. If the situation has deteriorated to the point where it requires a police presence, then the police must be in charge.

Here is a little trick that works pretty well. If the suspect is

The officer establishes psychological and a little physical dominace by standing on the curb to appear taller than the suspect.

standing in the street, you stand on the curb. If he is standing on the landing, you stand on the next step up. The idea is to establish a little height dominance and thus a little psychological superiority. It's worked more times than not for me.

Proper Attitude

We have all seen officers who walk into a calm situation and within minutes, turn everything to bedlam. They don't contribute to the resolution of a call because their bad attitude becomes part of the problem.

It's imperative that you not let your personal problems—such as ego, prejudices, or any other negative personal qualities—interfere or in any way affect how you perform your job. If you do, not only will you create more problems and possibly put your safety and others' at risk, but you will embarrass your agency and put it at risk of being held liable for your actions.

It is your personal responsibility to deal with your negative feelings. This can be done through introspection, counseling, discussions with peers and supervisors, meditation, and, in extreme cases, by removing yourself from the job.

You cannot solve problems for others if you can't get past your own.

Confidence

One of the largest factors in your success in a fight is your belief in your skill to take care of business. In karate, if you don't think your hand is going to slice cleanly through the brick, it won't. If you don't have the confidence to break a block of ice with your head, you are going to put a dent in your forehead large enough to fill with water for birds to bathe in.

Real confidence comes from knowledge and skill based on practice. Here is a simple statement that one of my martial arts teachers, Professor Remy Presas, is fond of quoting: "If you practice very hard, you will be very, very good." It's a short and simple declaration that states the truth about developing any skill, whether it is in the martial arts, police defensive tactics, or high school algebra.

False confidence is based on the erroneous assumption that you are able to apply your techniques in a real situation, though you haven't practiced them sufficiently. False confidence is dangerous since you may go into a situation that is over your head believing you have the skill to handle it.

The buzz words to having real confidence are "practice, practice, and, uh . . . oh yes—practice."

Control and Physical Force

You need to understand the differences and similarities between control and physical force, not only for your own guidance, but to enable you to articulate in court and to an Internal Affairs board why you did what you did.

Control may or may not require force. Most of the time, you can calm a volatile situation by being there in person with your pressed uniform and shiny bobbles. Other times it may require some words, even harsh words from you, to bring about quick order. And still other times, body positioning or just the touch of your hand will be all that it takes to bring quiet and calm to a situation.

Using force to bring about control can mean anything from employing a wristlock to firing a bullet into the suspect's forehead (the latter could be called "establishing control with extreme prejudice").

The amount of force used is determined by the degree to which the suspect is resisting or trying to hurt you. If you can establish control with a wristlock, fine. If it takes a bullet, then it takes a bullet. Be clear in your mind that you will use only the amount of force necessary to gain control. Know that if you use more force than is necessary, you open yourself up to criminal and civil liability. If you use less, you jeopardize your safety and the safety of others at the scene.

Chapter

3

The Nature of Fighting

I dragged myself into the locker room one night, nursing wounds suffered from a knock-down-drag-out fight with a speed freak who had been as determined not to go to jail as I was to take him there. As I was slipping out of my torn uniform shirt, painfully favoring my injured shoulder, an officer changing clothes at the next locker declared, "There isn't any reason police officers should get into fights with people out there."

My mouth must have dropped open for half a minute before I could ask him to repeat himself.

He sighed at my ignorance and rephrased his sentence. "I said, we don't need to fight these people. So much more good can be accomplished with intelligent dialog." He had been on the job two years.

I looked at him and wondered if he had ever been in a fight during his illustrious career, and if not, what had he been doing to avoid it. Luckily, he turned out to be good at promotional tests, made sergeant a few months later, and transferred to records—a fortunate move for officers on the street whose safety would have been jeopardized because of his stupid, naive philosophy.

We had a young rookie named Tiny who was, in fact, tiny. He had rosy cheeks, big, brown, doe-like eyes, a soft body, and a superior attitude, probably from growing up in an affluent family that had made life safe and rosy for him. Our winter uniform coats back then hung below our holsters, so it wasn't until the second or third week of working with Tiny that his coach discovered that the little dweeb had been putting his sidearm in the trunk of their police car at the beginning of each shift.

"I just don't want to ever have to use it," he later explained to the board of inquiry just before they fired him.

Gwendolyn was an intellectual with degrees in biology and philosophy. At 26 she already had life figured out; the problem was she hadn't lived it yet, she had only read about it in books. She had lots of ideas about police work, with big plans of making a monumental difference simply because she was involved in it.

She was an absolute pain in the butt in her academy's defensive tactics class, arguing with the instructors about every technique and every concept. The powers-that-be asked me to work with her and get her turned around, and although I tried, I couldn't make a dent. She even joined my private karate school, but she would insist on doing her own warm-ups and continually argued about my reasoning behind the various fighting techniques and drills. I finally got a clue one day to where her mind was when she commented, "I just can't accept the idea that there are people out there who want to hurt me, especially now that I'm a police officer." Hmm.

Three days later, she and her coach were confronted by a

man armed with a whirling chain saw. As her coach pointed his gun at the guy and pantomimed desperately for him to shut off the screaming death blades, Gwendolyn backed up several feet and began to—this is the absolute truth—file her nails. This was mental survival for her; it was her way of dealing with an abomination that in no way fit into her concept of reality. That's my Psychology 101 take of it, anyway.

Happily, she was fired a few days later.

The point of these three stories is that even with all the sophisticated psychological testing that my department uses, there are still some individuals who slip through and get hired. I know this happens in other police agencies, too. Even more amazing to me is that these people want to be police officers in the first place. With all the cop shows on television, cop buddy movies, magazine articles, and novels about police work, and all the bloody news stories on the news every night, how can they be so naive about the realities of the job? What on earth do they think it's about?

Let's put this question aside, since we will never get it answered anyway, and pose another one that has gnawed at me for years.

WHY DON'T OFFICERS WANT TO LEARN DEFENSIVE TACTICS?

Why don't police officers, veterans and rookies alike, want to participate in the best defensive tactics training they can get? Why are so many officers willing to spend hours, day after day, firing away at the range when, in the average career, they will get into dozens of empty-hand, resist arrest situations and maybe, just maybe, one shooting? The answer, of course, is that shooting is fun (and maybe a little sexual), and defensive tactics training is tiring and often painful.

The reality is that police officers are going to get into fights.

People resist arrest, mentally
deranged people flip out, and
cop haters attack police officers. Some patrol areas are
quiet places where physical
confrontations are rare, while
other districts are so nasty that
even the most passive officers
find themselves tumbling
about on the sidewalk two or
three times a week. The bottom line is that uniformed
officers working the street are
inevitably going to get into a
fight. It may be nothing more
than a suspect stiffening his
arm as handcuffs are applied,
or it may be a slugfest straight
out of a John Wayne movie.

*The officer is focusing all of his atten-
tion on the suspect's stiff arm and is
oblivious to the other arm that is out
of sight.*

The unknown entity in
every physical encounter is the
motivation and objective be-
hind the resistance. Is the suspect stiffening his arm just to defy
your authority, or is he setting you up to get at your weapon, or at
his? If you are in a toe-to-toe fistfight with a guy, is he doing it to
get at your gun, or is he doing it because he just wants to punch
the crap out of a police officer with no intention of taking it any
further? Does the suspect even know what his motivation is? How
many times have you heard a suspect say something like, "I didn't
mean for that to happen. I didn't intend for it to go that far"?

The answer is that you don't know, nor will you ever know,
what a resisting person's motivation is, any more than you can
ever be certain about what you are walking up on when you make
a traffic stop. Therefore, because of this unknown factor, you
must consider every physical force situation serious. Whether you
are involved in a passive resistance situation or a violent slugfest,
the potential for it to turn deadly is always just a hair breadth

away. If that doesn't make you take your defensive tactics training seriously, then you should get out of the business. You would be better off selling greeting cards at a Hallmark store. Let's look at what I call the nature of fighting—what it is and what it isn't. Let's examine some commonly held myths about training and fighting, ways to think about fighting to win, ways to be mentally aware, and ways to think survival when a slow, boring shift suddenly explodes and turns bloody.

COMMONLY HELD MYTHS
ABOUT DEFENSIVE TACTICS

Listed below are a few beliefs held by far too many officers about defensive tactics training and fighting. Are any of them yours?

1. *My agency's defensive tactics program provides all the techniques and training I need to handle every physical force situation.* No one program can train you for every situation you encounter on the street because there are always surprises in a fight, things you never thought would happen. It's important, therefore, that you are aware of your training's strengths and weaknesses. Do all that you can to eliminate, or at least minimize, those weaknesses, but understand that realistically you can't get rid of them all. Assess the many possible situations you might get into where those weak points could raise their ugly heads and then take every precaution you can to avoid getting into them.

2. *Officers who get hurt in a fight screwed up somewhere.* Not true at all. If the suspect is bigger, faster, tougher, and gets the jump on the officer first, even the best-trained officer in defensive tactics will come out second best. Skill in defensive tactics only provides you with an edge; it does not turn an officer into Superman. Even if the officer and the suspect are comparable in their skill levels, someone has to lose. That is one big reason you should do everything you can to avoid resorting to physical force.

3. *A highly trained police officer can work without fear and doesn't need to take precautions.* I hope that you think this statement is ridiculous. Fear warns us of dangerous situations and tells us to be cautious and use specific tactics. A highly trained officer knows his limitations and knows how far his skill can take him. He knows there are always people out there, people who have never had a minute of training, who can nonetheless kick his butt. He takes precautions because he is trained.

4. *Defensive tactic techniques are designed to overcome suspects who are physically larger and physically superior.* This is true, sort of. If the suspect is superior because he is armed, then he indeed has a strong advantage. Yes, there are lots of effective disarming tactics in existence, but conditions have to be strongly in your favor before they will work successfully. You need proper distancing, precision timing, lightning speed, quick reflexes, and a cool demeanor (as a fellow officer once said, "It's hard to disarm someone when you are slipping on your own shit").

    According to history, many martial arts were designed to fight occupying armies. However, they often had to fight empty-handed, and though they won some individual fights, no occupied country ever defeated its oppressors.

    There can be a problem when a larger person is trained in the fighting arts, too. All things being equal, the bigger fighter has an edge over the smaller fighter.

5. *Your defensive tactics should be used only when you are attacked.* Well, there are plenty of nitwit citizens who believe this and not just a few police administrators. Have you ever noticed how those people who come up with goofy beliefs and goofy rules are those people who will never have to worry about personally testing them?

    You can't apply your nifty defensive tactics if the suspect punches your lights out first. I don't know about you, but I don't get paid enough to wait to be attacked and then apply my defensive tactics. What if your reflexes are slow that day, or what if the suspect is a superior fighter? The problem is that you don't know the answer to these questions until the fight starts, and then it just might be too late. If the situation warrants it, you need to act first.

Of course, there is always one student who asks: "If defensive tactics are martial arts, aren't you supposed to use them for defense only?" I answer by pointing at my mug. "See this handsome face," I say humbly. "You notice there aren't any marks on it? Twenty-nine years of police work, and thirty some years of martial arts training, and not one mark. You want to know why? Cause I always attack first."

6. *Having knowledge of defensive tactics is the same as being able to use them.* This is one of the biggest myths there is in police defensive tactics and why so many officers have problems applying their techniques on the street. Their knowledge doesn't translate into skill at applying them in real situations where suspects are resisting, bystanders are screaming, sirens are blaring, and the stress and tension needle is blipping into the red zone.

I can teach an officer how to do a wristlock in five minutes, but his knowledge is only superficial. It has not yet been ingrained into his subconscious mind, and for that matter, after five minutes it's barely into his conscious mind. Techniques must be practiced over and over, and then, over one more time. Yes, you can know a technique after a few minutes, but you will never *know* it until you practice it hundreds of times.

The late karate master Mas Oyama, known for killing a bull with a single punch (which he has done more than 50 times), said that you don't truly know a technique until you have done it 300,000 times (imagine that training budget).

7. *Practicing defensive tactic drills will make me an expert.* It is a good start, but you need to do more. You need to think deeply about what you are doing. As you physically practice your techniques, you need to ask yourself the following questions:

- Why am I doing this?
- Why am I using this technique in this situation?

- Why am I standing this way?
- What if the suspect moves while I am doing this?
- What if this technique fails?
- What are the suspect's strong points?
- How can I do this better?
- Is there a better technique that applies here?

Your thinking process, your mental attitude, and your self-evaluation are just as important as your physical training. Combine these elements with intelligence, and you will be much stronger than if you only practiced physically.

8. *Defensive tactics training will transform every officer into a great fighter.* Quality defensive tactics training will certainly help every officer do better on the street. Other factors, however, such as genetics, natural ability, physical strength, mental discipline, the ability to perform well under stress, intelligence, personality, and continued hard training will all contribute to an officer's fighting ability.

9. *An officer trained in defensive tactics can probably defend himself.* As mentioned before, a trained officer will have a better chance of defending himself than an officer who has not had defensive tactics training. Training provides you with an edge, an increased level of skill that will help you in an "average" arrest. There is no amount of training that will help you defend against a surprise attack, an ambush that seemingly comes out of nowhere. If you are taken by surprise and you don't get a chance to put up a fight, all your cool techniques are useless.

10. *You can tell by a person's appearance whether he is going to be a good fighter.* Wrong, wrong, wrong. You absolutely cannot tell by looking at someone how formidable he will be in a fight. As a military policeman in Vietnam, I had to arrest Green Beret soldiers on a couple of occasions. These men are elite fighters who are trained in a variety of skills. Most of them are as hard as nails, with pumped muscles and protruding veins in their foreheads. Both times I was ready for the fight of my life, but both times the Green Berets broke down and cried like little children.

On the other hand, I have had 10-year-old children fight like savages. I wear a one-inch scar on my thumb where a 65-year-old woman kicked me, and a skinny teenager nearly pushed me through a plate-glass window. An international bodybuilding champion, who has graced the cover of many muscle magazines, once locked himself in his bathroom and cried and begged my partner, who was about as big as the pumper's thigh, not to hurt him. At karate tournaments, I've seen geeky-looking competitors effortlessly kick the dog doo-doo out of their opponents, and I've seen 70-year-old martial arts masters throw young and hungry black belts around like Frisbees.

Never, never, never underestimate anyone.

One objective of this book is to get you thinking about how to make your defensive tactics training better. Know that skill in physical tactics is both physical and mental, requiring lots of practice beyond what you get in the academy and at in-service training. It will not turn you into Superman, nor will it make you invulnerable. It will give you an edge, a slight advantage over the average fighter.

It is always to your advantage to avoid a fight, to avoid using force unless absolutely necessary.

Let's look at several facets that make up the nature of fighting.

DEALING WITH FEAR

Much of your fear comes from a lack of confidence in your abilities to handle a stressful situation, such as taking a big, hairy-knuckled slob out of a tavern when he doesn't want to leave. For sure, there will be stress no matter how good your tactics, because there are always surprises that can screw up even the best plans. "The best plans turn to shit as soon as the shooting starts," we said in Vietnam. Nonetheless, the better trained you are, the higher your confidence and the more in control you are of your anxiety.

Here are a few elements that when acquired will greatly reduce your fear level.

1. *Master defensive tactics techniques, concepts, and principles.*
2. *Think about potentially fearful situations.*
   - Anticipate that you will get into a fight.
   - Think about a variety of situations where you will use physical force.
   - Think about how the situations can go down and what problems can occur.
   - Think about your current skill level in defensive tactics and how it relates to the particulars of the various situations. Where do you need to improve?
3. *Understand and accept the effects of fear.*
   - Don't think of fear as negative, but as a positive warning device that keeps you alert and prepares you to survive. Fear can make you sharp, ready, and strong.
4. *Learn controlled breathing techniques.*
   - These are not some new-age gobbledygook, but proven and easy-to-do techniques that will calm you in seconds.
5. *Read* Deadly Force Encounters.
   - This book, which was written by Alexis Artwohl and me (published by Paladin Press), has a large section on understanding and dealing with fear.
6. *Stay physically fit.*
   - A strong, healthy body will give you confidence and a strong, healthy outlook. When you are fit, you are more motivated and receptive to analyzing all the elements in a potentially stressful situation, and you will do well when it goes down. Being fit will provide you with the strength and energy reserves to fight well and survive.
7. *Develop a winning mind-set.*
   - Have no doubt in your mind that you will come out on top of every fight you engage in. Know in your mind that you will absolutely, positively gain control of the suspect, get him handcuffed, and get him into the backseat of your car. No doubt whatsoever. Period.

Once you have developed skill in defensive tactics techniques, understand the many possible situations in which a fight can erupt. Understand that fear can actually be a positive force. With a greater understanding of yourself, you will keep your anxiety level down and controlled and your energy focused on what needs to be done.

WINNING IS EVERYTHING

I discussed earlier that you should never consider a fight a game or some kind of competition. A lot of bad guys believe that it is, and so do far too many police officers. Yes, thrashing about with some greasy low-life maggot is part of your career choice, but it's work—it's *never* competition.

Nonetheless, you have to think of it in terms of doing whatever you have to do to win, to come out on top. You have to stop thinking in terms of "playing" within the rules set by your agency and the statutes. You have to stop thinking in terms of limitations and that it's more important how you play than whether you win. Winning is everything when fighting a suspect. How can it not be when your personal safety and the safety of others are at stake?

A Brief War Story

One morning I spotted old John Lee pushing his grocery cart along the skidrow sidewalk, just as I had seen him do every day for years. John Lee was a wino like most of the row's inhabitants, an old man who spent his days cruising with his cart and occasionally pilfering a baseball hat from straight citizens who left their cars unlocked.

Every day I would ask him the same question: "Hey, John Lee. Where'd you get that hat?" And every day he would answer the same way: "Gott-damnit copper, it's yur mama's hat. I gots it from your sweet mama."

This day, as my partner and I strolled by him, I asked my usual question, but instead of his usual answer, he assumed a boxer's stance and took a wild swing at me. I was surprised, though I didn't feel threatened since he missed me by a mile. I glanced over at my partner and smiled at her, indicating that I was going to play with old John Lee a little. I assumed a boxer's stance and bobbed and weaved for a second, then looked back at my partner to see if she was laughing.

She wasn't. Her eyes suddenly widened as she looked past me toward the old man. I jerked my head toward John Lee just as my partner lunged past me and grabbed his arm. Clutched tightly in his fist was a three-foot long stick with several nails protruding like shark's teeth from its end. In the brief moment I had turned to look at my partner, the old man had snatched the deadly weapon from his grocery cart and cocked it over his shoulder like a crazy baseball batter. My partner grabbed it just as he began whipping it toward my face.

I had been playing a game with old John Lee, but the old man's burned-out brain wasn't seeing it that way. Lucky for me, my partner wasn't either.

Police work is not a game. If you think it is, you dramatically increase the daily risk.

Playing by the Rules Can Get Your Butt Bit

As police officers, we do just about everything by the rules. In my agency the rules are called G.O.s, general orders, and it's a massive book, practically a foot thick. We are so conditioned to play by the rules that often we put our safety at risk because we are uncomfortable, even afraid, to break them.

In the late 1970s, someone in my agency came up with the harebrained idea of placing a strip of masking tape over the pump action on every officer's shotgun. The "thinking" was that a broken tape at the end of the officer's shift would reveal that he had, for whatever reason, chambered a round during his tour. The shift sergeant would see this and order the officer to write a report about why he'd done it.

This order lasted for only a few months before it was rescinded. The administration finally realized that this simple piece of tape placed a psychological "stop point" in the officers' minds. In fact, there is a war story about an officer who lost his life because of his agency's requirement to tape their shotgun slides. The tape caused the officer to hesitate just long enough for the suspect to act first, and the officer died with his shotgun slide still taped.

If a little piece of tape can cause hesitation, what do all the rules do? For one thing, they cause us to act with limitations, as if it were more important how we play than whether we win. This is crazy. Why should it be more important that we obey every little rule, rather than doing whatever has to be done to survive the situation?

Andrew J. Casavant, in an article called "Winning Isn't Everything: It's the Only Thing," published in *The Police Marksman*, wrote, "These days, it seems that winning is not as important as losing graciously. I hear parents tell their kids, 'Don't worry about winning, just go have fun. After all, winning isn't as important as being a good sport.' What kind of an attitude encourages kids to lose and then accept it as more important than winning just because they played a good sport? Subsequently, we have created a generation of good losers and poor winners."

Are we training police officers to be good losers, or are we training them to be winners? Is obeying that thick rule book more important, or are there situations where officers must throw the book to the wind, break the damn rules, and do whatever it takes to get home at the end of the shift? I hope this is an easy question for you to answer.

At the risk of sounding like an old fart, I sometimes wonder about the new generation of police officers getting hired. When I came on in 1972, there were still a few officers on who had been in World War II and many who had served in the Korean War. Most of my peers who were hired two or three years before me and five or six years after me, had been in Vietnam or at least in the military. That is not so today. Today officers are getting hired right out of college and out of President Clinton's Police Corps program, with very little life experience. Recently, I heard a young recruit tell his buddy that a citizen had yelled at him. The officer said he was shocked because he had never been around conflict like that and never been in a physical confrontation of any kind.

There are lots of these sheltered men and women getting hired today. Does this mean they are not going to do a good job? Not at all. But it does mean they are going to have a greater time adjusting to the realities of police work than did the last few generations of officers who had been in the military and fought in wars.

New officers are being hired today because they fit into the community policing mold. They are nonconfrontational and politically correct, not concerned with winning, but with playing the game properly. But when they are thrust out into the cold, wet streets of reality, they become confused. How can they maintain their correct look, say all the correct things, do everything correctly for their community-policing-oriented agency, when they are getting their butts kicked?

I am not criticizing the new officers; I am just concerned for their safety. They must be taught from the very beginning to win—that the job of policing often requires them to use force and that there is nothing wrong with using it to get the job done. They need to understand that having to use force doesn't mean they did something wrong; sometimes it's the only option.

Officers must be taught that winning is everything. Think of it this way. What if you have been taken hostage by a couple of armed holdup men? Wouldn't you want your rescuers to have one thought in their minds: to set you free? You would not want a squad of SWAT officers concerned with playing well. You would want them to win and do so quickly. You would want them to have one dominant objective: to win, win, win.

Officers often complain that their administration does not praise them when they win. When an officer gets into a blazing shoot-out in the street, say a white officer in a minority neighborhood, most police administrations are more concerned about how the shooting looks politically than the fact the officer won the fight. If you have a chief who goes on television and says he is proud of how his officer performed in a nasty, politically sensitive shooting, and that he is glad the suspect lost and the officer won, you have a chief who should be worshipped.

I won most of my trophies in karate competition after I turned 40. My goal was to continue competing into my 50s, just so I could say that I did it. But when I was 44, I injured my pectorals and shoulder so seriously in a fight on a skidrow street corner that it brought my competitive career to a screaming halt. A big part of me was disappointed that I could no longer enter tournaments, but in a way I was OK with it, too.

For about a year before I was injured, I was having trouble getting myself motivated to compete. I have always trained hard, and, in fact, there have often been times when I have needed discipline not to train, like when I was sick or physically exhausted. But I was beginning to feel a lack of desire to compete, do the specialized training needed, travel, and suffer through the competition anxiety. My hunger for it waned each time I competed, and I would always ask myself, "Why am I still doing this?" If I hadn't been injured, I'm not sure what I would have done. Most likely my lack of desire would have started to show in my performance.

That was competition, sport, fun. The street is not any of those things. You must instill in yourself—and if you are an instructor, in your students—a desire to win and a mind-set that it's not OK to lose in the concrete reality of the street. You must accept that there is no shame in winning, that it's your responsibility to win, to yourself, your fellow officers, your family, and the public you serve. Yes, there are rules, laws, and general orders that dictate how you do your job, but when it comes to life and death, you must not let these things put up a wall and block you from doing what you've got to do to survive.

It is true that one of the big changes happening today is that police agencies are hiring more politically correct, nonconfrontational people to do the job. Although that may be a big change from just a few years ago, what has remained constant is that the street is still the same—it's full of assholes. If these humanistic-type officers fail to approach the job with a winning attitude, then they will lose—and losing can really hurt.

Winning feels a lot better.

KILLER INSTINCT

This subsection could also fit into the survival chapter, but I have decided to include it here because it ties in with the section "Winning Is Everything."

When I was in the army during the Vietnam era, we trained to kill "dinks," "gooks," "slopes," "slants," "VC," "noodle suckers," or "yellow bastards," as the North Vietnamese were often derogatively called. During World War II, American soldiers fought the "krauts" and "Jap bastards." The Japanese called Americans "barbarians." Every army in every war has names for the enemy for one primary reason: to dehumanize them and make them easier to kill.

We can argue all day long about whether we are in a war out on the streets. Are criminals poor unfortunates who are acting out because they were abused as children, or are they an enemy force that we need to strike at with everything we have? Well, let's leave such pondering to the psychologists, social workers, bleeding hearts, and others who have the luxury of thinking about such things from the safety of their offices and meeting rooms.

Right now we are concerned about coming out on top in a fight. To that end, it's important that you hold this philosophy: when engaged in a fight for personal survival with a criminal, you must fight all-out. You must fight to win. You must fight to stop the suspect, even if it means killing him.

One method that works for some officers is to mentally dehumanize the suspect who has attacked them so that they can fight with greater intensity. I am not suggesting that you look at the suspect through eyes filled with racial, ethnic, religious, sexual orientation, or gender prejudice. On the other hand, I am not saying that you *shouldn't* take that approach (boy, won't the piously indignant cop watchers have a field day with this concept?).

You have to look into yourself to decide what you must do to bring out that politically incorrect term *killer instinct*. When you are defending your life, you cannot fight with limitations, you cannot hold back for reasons of etiquette, a sense of humanity, personal religious reasons, or fear of Internal Affairs or of being sued. If you are absolutely convinced that you are fighting for your life, you owe it to yourself and your family to use whatever personal psychological ploy that helps you get the job done. If that means you have to view the suspect as a rabid junkyard dog, so be it.

When the suspect attacks you with viciousness, you must fight back with greater viciousness. Why would you do anything less? For sure, this is not a topic you would discuss at a community meeting or a woman's canasta club. These people would never understand because it's too far removed from their reality.

It is, however, your reality. As a police officer, you patrol the streets to maintain peace and harmony. But when you or an innocent person in your presence is attacked with viciousness, you must respond with the same, albeit with an objective of getting control. Don't doubt that the killer instinct is there, even in the woosiest, Milquetoast, bow-tie-wearing, new-age cop. He might have to dig a little deeper, but for sure he will find it. It's a cold entity, but it's also energy producing. It will make you stronger, faster, and resistant to pain.

And it will help you get home at the end of your shift.

STAY RELAXED

To fight at your best, you need to be relaxed. But how can you when a hairy-knuckled ape is trying to rip your eye out of its socket? Here are a few positive attributes that will help you relax as much as possible when the poop hits the fan.

1. *Have confidence in your physical techniques.* Confidence is developed as a result of training sufficiently to ingrain the techniques into your conscious and subconscious mind and into your muscle memory. By thoroughly practicing your techniques, you not only develop a complete understanding of how they work but a deep understanding of your ability to apply them.

2. *Be mentally prepared to fight.* It's important that you accept the possibility that you may be called on at any time to fight, and fight hard. Accept that you might get hurt and that you will continue to fight no matter how grave your injuries. If

you don't consider this possibility, and it happens to you, you may be so shocked that you won't be able to physically respond. I've seen it happen to some very big guys.

3. *Learn to monitor and control your breathing.* As you race through the night on a hot call, be cognizant of taking breaths through your nose, drawing the oxygen deep into your belly, holding it there for a few seconds, and then slowly blowing it out. If you don't control your breathing, anxiety will cause you to breathe shallowly into your upper chest, which can add to your stress and quickly deplete your energy and strength.

Try this breathing method right now. Sit up straight and inhale through your nose for about a 10 count, hold for another 10 count, and then exhale slowly out your mouth. Repeat until you begin to feel relaxed, a calming sensation that usually begins to wash over you after about six exchanges. Feels good, doesn't it? If you want to learn about other breathing methods, check out my book *The Way Alone*, available from Paladin Press.

The more you practice your breathing exercises, the easier it will be for you to apply controlled breathing under pressure. I did it once when I was facing more than 100 protesters and my backup was five minutes away. I did it subtly so that no one noticed even as I stood blocking their entrance into an abortion clinic. After a few seconds, my anxiety was reduced, and I could control the crowd with carefully chosen words until other officers arrived.

Police officers don't have the luxury of running away from a dangerous situation. Citizens can take flight, but they pay us the big bucks to stay. Still, the fight-or-flight reflex can still happen to us. To resist the urge to take flight, concentrate all your attention on the task that needs to be done. Don't acknowledge the natural instinct to back off (unless, of course, that is the best strategy for the situation). Stay in there and use whatever force the situation calls for. Concentrate on your objective, which is usually to take control of the situation.

WHEN A SUSPECT ASSUMES A FIGHTING STANCE

While most of the time a suspect will resist arrest by stiffening his arms, there are times when he puts up his dukes and makes it clear that he wants to fight you. Let's look at a few concepts taught in the martial arts and see how they adapt to police defensive tactics.

Never Fight Your Opponent's Fight

If the suspect puts up his dukes, don't put up yours. If he gets into a wrestler's crouch, don't you get into a wrestler's crouch. If he looks like he's a kicker, don't you fight him with your kicks.

Whatever stance a suspect assumes, he most likely does so because he feels comfortable with it. If he assumes a hands-up, boxerlike stance, it's because he has been training to fight that way, or if not, at least it's the most natural way for him to fight. Keep in mind that just because he hasn't been trained with his hands doesn't mean he can't get lucky with them and trash your nose.

If a guy assumes a high stance and begins moving his legs as if preparing to kick, you should assume that he has been trained somewhat to fight with his legs. His training may have consisted of only a week at the local shopping mall's taekwon do school, or it may have been for 20 years as he grew up with the tongs in China where his father worked for the American Embassy. You just don't know. But you do know that he is at least thinking in terms of using his feet.

If he crouches like a wrestler, you should assume he is a grappler. He may have had a week of it as a child at his local community recreation center, he may be the state collegiate wrestling champion, or he may be a 5th-degree black belt in jujitsu. Again, you don't know. What you do know is that he is thinking in terms of grappling with you.

In my karate school, I teach that if a guy assumes a boxer's stance, you blast his legs with hard kicks. If he assumes a kicking stance, you jam him, punch him in the body, and elbow him in the face. If he assumes a grappling stance, you should stay light on your feet and move quickly in and out of range, delivering quick kicks to his legs and snap punches to his extended arms and hands.

The point is that you don't fight the other guy's fight since he is probably good at it, or at least he thinks he is good at fighting in that area (and just thinking he is good can make him good to some degree).

As a police officer using defensive tactics, your choices are easier. Anytime a suspect assumes a fighting stance, he has established the rules of the fight, which are these: He gets into a fighting stance, and you spray him with pepper or smash him with your baton. It doesn't get much easier than that, though you should still be aware of what stance he is in.

I like to hit grapplers on their extended hands with my baton. Against a kicker, I move in quickly with my side toward him to protect my groin and jam his legs. Against boxers, I like to hit their dukes with my baton or strike at their legs. A burst of pepper spray is nice, too, because it can get right past their high-guard position.

Remember, police work is not a game where you have to fight by archaic "gentlemen's" rules. You have a job to do, and the job is to take the suspect into custody. That doesn't mean "let's have an equal fight here and see who comes out on top." That's nonsense, it's dangerous, and it's not what police work is about. It's about getting the job of physical force done quickly, efficiently, and safely.

When the subject assumes a fighting stance, no matter what the stance, you don't want to get into a one-on-one with him if you're empty handed. If he gets into a stance and backs away a little, rest your hand on your baton or spray canister and order him to stop, turn around, and interlace his fingers behind his head. But if he assumes a stance and moves toward you, pull your weapon, sidestep, and hit him with a burst of spray or a baton strike across his shins.

The Element of Surprise
The element of surprise always works in your favor, so don't

give away your intentions. Don't posture with your pepper can and warn him that you are going to spray, because you give him the opportunity to think about a defense. Don't retrieve your baton from its holder, cock it over your shoulder, and give him that killer stare of yours. Again, you will have provided him with the opportunity to formulate a plan. However . . .

Dazzle Him with a Cool Pose

Sometimes a threatening posture will work. I used to carry an aluminum baton in a metal ring (my favorite of all the fancy-schmancy batons on the market). On several occasions I drew it quick as a wink, which made a pronounced metallic sound as the baton slid against the ring. Then I gave the baton a twirl in my hand and dropped into a cool fighting pose. The three or four times I did this little schtick, the suspects always held up their hands and said something like, "OK, OK, you win. Take me."

I hesitate to tell you this because while it worked every time I took the chance, who knows if it would have worked the next time. If you want to try it, first carefully judge the circumstances of the situation. For example, if the suspect is in a fighting stance and backing away from you, and there is no avenue of escape and no potential weapons available, that may be a time that it will work. Then again it may not. Only you can judge, so use it at your own risk. I didn't tell you to do it. So don't sue me.

Chapter
4
Training

WHO ARE THE INSTRUCTORS?

This is what all too often occurs in police agencies, especially larger ones. The defensive tactics instructor has studied a martial art of some kind, maybe a little, maybe a lot, and has volunteered or been forced into teaching defensive tactics. If he needs assistance, he recruits one or more other officers to coinstruct with him. Of those, one will have a little background in a martial art, while the others do not.

Even if an instructor has martial arts experience, it may or may not relate to police defensive tactics. For example, if the instructor is a black belt in taekwon do or kung fu, his skill may not be applicable to the needs of police work since only a few instructors in these fighting arts teach joint-locking techniques. It's been my experience that even when an officer has earned a couple of black belts in a martial art that doesn't have grappling techniques, teaching him defensive tactics is no different from teaching an officer who has had no martial arts training at all. In fact, sometimes it's harder to teach him because he is preconditioned to react in a way in which police officers should not react—such as kicking a suspect in the chops.

Far too many defensive tactics programs are taught by officers who have no background in the martial arts. As a result, they teach only what they have been taught to teach or what they devise from books, videos, and a couple of defensive tactics seminars. This works as long as there are no technical questions from students, no complex "what ifs . . . ." But what happens when there are questions that go beyond what the instructor knows?

Unfortunately, many instructors, in an attempt not to look ignorant in front of their students, will answer with misinformed or completely inaccurate information. When this happens, students lose confidence in the instructor. After all, police officers get lied to all day long by the public. As a result, they have excellent bullshit detectors when it comes to reading people who are not being straightforward with them. Even if an instructor does it only once, it will still take him a long time, if ever, to regain respect and confidence from his students.

A greater problem occurs when an instructor gives poor or improper information that could get an officer hurt. Instruction that teaches dangerous survival skills and body mechanics can put an officer at risk.

In contrast, an instructor who has a pertinent martial arts background and can relate it to defensive tactics can better explain why something isn't working, how to make it work, and what nuances are needed to adapt it to different situations and environments. Additionally, this instructor can decide if it's the best technique for that specific officer, given his height, weight, and so on.

Techniques tend to get watered down when they are taught by instructors with limited knowledge and experience. This can be seen in martial arts systems that hand out black belts to people after only two years of instruction and then place them in teaching positions. I find this absurd. A new black belt, especially a two-year wonder, should be given only limited teaching responsibilities, and even then he should be watched and critiqued by an experienced instructor.

This is what happens with defensive tactics instructors whose backgrounds are limited to only what they were taught by an instructor whose knowledge was also limited. Would a police agency turn over a major crime scene to a rookie? Of course not. So why are instructors with limited knowledge given the responsibility of teaching police officers handcuffing techniques and self-defense?

The Ideal Instructor

So what is the solution? Well, because of the problems of agency budgets, time constraints, manpower shortages, and blockheaded administrators, a realistic solution is also a fantasy solution that would have to be placed into the last section of this book, "Dream List," since it will never happen. But you asked, so here is what I think needs to be done.

Every police agency needs to get defensive tactics instructors who have an extensive background in some kind of grappling martial art, such as aikido, chin-na, jujitsu, judo, or wrestling. Although taekwon do, karate, and kung fu are great punch- or kickfighting arts, instructors trained in them will have little to offer unless they have also been trained in grappling skills. Additionally, instructors need to be police officers because they need to know the specific needs of law enforcement and how to modify ancient grappling moves into modern-day police techniques.

Yes, this is idealistic, but it's the best solution to the problem.

Before we leave this section, let me just add that I have seen some excellent instructors who demonstrated patience and understanding of the material, could recognize students' problems, and had the knowledge to correct errors. Nonetheless, their knowledge was limited because they did not have an extensive background in the martial arts. Eventually they would be asked questions they couldn't answer.

NONAPPLICABLE TECHNIQUES

Allow me to mention one other thing before we get into the training ideas. Let's discuss briefly the issue of nonapplicable techniques. As mentioned before in this book, there are hundreds of grappling techniques among the assorted fighting arts. There are many that cause excruciating pain to the recipient; some that dislocate joints, break bones, and tear muscles and tendons; and some that are designed to kill. But while there are many effective and brutal techniques, there are only a few that are applicable to the routine needs of daily law enforcement work.

Young officers are always coming to me and suggesting a "new" technique they think is the answer to all their fighting needs. First, understand that there are few new techniques. One might have come to them in a dream or evolved out of the material they were working on, but believe me, it already exists somewhere in a fighting system. Secondly, nine times out of ten, the new technique does not fit the unique needs of police work. Here is a good example.

An officer recently showed me a move that he thought was cool because it hurt his brother-in-law at their family picnic. To apply it, you reach out and grab the suspect by his right wrist. You lift his arm as you step next to him, then you stretch it across your shoulders, behind your head, rotate his palm so it faces upward to lock his elbow joint, and then you pull down on his wrist. With his elbow now hyperextended on your shoulders and your other hand around his waist, you can escort the guy on his tiptoes out the door.

The problem is this: you can't handcuff him from this position. Yes, you can make him cry uncle and cry for his mother, but you can't put on the cuffs without giving up the technique and starting all over. A skilled jujitsu fighter could do it, but there is no easy way to teach nonmartial-artist police officers how to transition from that position to the handcuff position with the suspect's hands behind his back. That's what I mean about the unique requirements of law enforcement.

Yes, this is a painful technique, but how can the suspect be handcuffed from this position?

So, why apply a hold if you are going to have to give up the pain-compliance part of it to move the suspect's arms to where his wrists can be handcuffed? Doesn't it make sense to use techniques that place the suspect in a position to be handcuffed from the very get-go? Yes it does.

The exception to this rule happens when you are engaged in a fight to survive, as we will discuss in a later chapter. In that situation, you use whatever it takes to get the suspect under control; then when you have help from other officers, you can transition him into a position to be cuffed. But for so-called routine resist situations, choose techniques that place the suspect into a position to be handcuffed as part of the procedure.

TEACHING IT TO LEARN IT BETTER

Teaching is an effective way to learn. In many martial arts' schools, students who have earned a colored belt are given some minor instruction duties. Yellow belt is the first belt earned in my school, a rank that takes about three months. If a yellow belt has a particularly good kick, for example, I'll have him teach it to a beginner. I monitor his teaching, of course, to ensure that he doesn't come up with an off-the-wall explanation, but I let him teach the entire movement. Afterward I might further explain some aspect of the technique to the beginner, but for the most part, I want the yellow belt to get the experience of teaching.

Teaching forces you to think about the elements of a movement and articulate them so that other people understand. This is not easy for everyone to do, but it's worth the effort to learn because it will dramatically improve understanding of the technique.

Several years ago, I went through a week-long FBI shooting school for instructors. The week was spent learning an assortment of stances and techniques and afforded us the opportunity to shoot a variety of weapons. Then the last two days were spent teaching our classmates what we had learned.

Everyone partnered up and formed a line in front of the targets. The student/officer would then pretend that he didn't know a thing about shooting and the teacher/officer would talk the student through the positions, step by step. We were told by the FBI instructors to avoid vague words and sentences and to articulate as clearly as possible. If the teacher/officer said something vague or unclear, the student/officer was to do exactly what he said or to ask for a better explanation. For example, if the instruction was to "shoot with your strong eye," the student would ask, "What? I don't shoot with the gun?" Although this may seem silly, the idea was to get everyone thinking about articulating the various techniques as clearly and completely as possible. This not only taught officers to be good instructors, it was an invaluable way to ingrain the material into their minds.

Teaching Defensive Tactics

When I'm teaching defensive tactics and there is enough time, I'll have the students teach each other a technique that we've been drilling on. Say we have been working on the prone handcuffing procedure and have come to a point where everyone looks good. I then have them form into groups of three, one student on his stomach to be handcuffed, one student to do the handcuffing, and one to teach the procedure. The student applying the handcuffs will act as if he has never seen the procedure before and does only what the instructor tells him to do. Not only does the teacher benefit from the exercise, but the other two students benefit from hearing the explanation from other people. After the three students have rotated through the three roles three of four times, their skill level and their understanding of the many fine points of the technique improve dramatically.

Students like this exercise, and they always remark that they learned even more about the techniques after teaching it several times. A nice side benefit is that often I hear students explain a phase of a technique better than the way I was explaining it. The teacher learns from the student.

COMMONALITY OF TRAINING

When I was a rookie in the police academy, our defensive tactics training consisted of four one-hour sessions of come-along holds and a few judo breakfalls (an appropriate name if you fall incorrectly) on a rock-hard mat. We were taught techniques for moving a suspect from point A to point B, more techniques for getting a suspect out of a chair, more to get him into the chair, two to get him into the police car, and two or three to get him out. All these techniques were different. They were all good, viable ones, but we were taught so many of them that we could barely remember more than one or two a week later. There were so many in such a short time that our retention just went out the window.

Instructors often teach too many techniques because they haven't considered the issue of retention, or they tell their students to try all the techniques, then choose one or two that they like. This shotgun approach to teaching is not an efficient use of class time, and to make matters even worse, the techniques usually lack commonality.

I define "commonality of training" as teaching techniques

  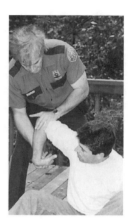

The common police flex technique can be used in a variety of situations, for example, as a come-along hold, which forces the suspect up onto his toes. When the officer slips his left arm to the outside of the suspect's arm, it forces the suspect down. By rolling the suspect's arm over and applying pressure, the pain encourages the suspect to stand.

that can be used in a variety of situations. When I began training in the martial arts, I learned a defensive block for a straight kick, another block for a round kick, another for a hook, and yet another for a side kick. I did a passable job executing the variety of blocks when I was just a white and a colored belt and training with other white and colored belts. But when I got higher in rank and tried to block kicks thrown by black belts, some of whom had kicks that were quick as a wink and powerful as a battering ram, I discovered that I didn't have enough time to choose the right block. Later, when I had my own school, I eliminated the choices. We now block all kicks, circular and straight, with the same block. This made the blocker's response time faster because there was less confusion over which choices to make.

Whether you are a defensive tactics instructor or a student, you should strive to make your tactics as versatile as possible. A physical force situation can erupt in an instant, sometimes explosively. This is not conducive for complicated tactics or ones that require lengthy decision-making. The greater your ability to adapt a minimum of techniques to a variety of situations, the greater your chance will be that you will come out on top.

Let's look at a police control hold usually referred to as a police wrist lock. While this is commonly taught as a control technique to move a suspect a short distance, it can actually be used in several situations.

- To move a suspect a short distance
- To force a suspect to stand up from a chair
- To put a suspect in a car
- To remove a suspect from a car
- To pick a suspect up from the floor
- To take a suspect down to the floor
- To use as a pain compliance hold to gain control of a suspect
- To use as a control hold when applying handcuffs

Logic dictates that it's better to have one technique for 10 situations than 10 different techniques for 10 situations. But before this can happen, you have to know just how versatile a given technique can be. So how is this knowledge found? Two ways:

1. Through a qualified martial arts instructor, especially one trained in jujitsu or other grappling arts
2. Through experimentation

A good grappling instructor will know the versatility of a given technique and can show variations applicable to law enforcement needs. If the police instructor is an experienced grappler, the issue is solved. If he isn't, he should seek out additional information about the techniques he is teaching with a good grappling instructor.

The other way to gain knowledge about a technique, though it's not as good as learning from a qualified martial artist, is to experiment. This is usually done by brainstorming with other instructors to examine a variety of scenarios to determine if the technique can be used in them. I have always found this to be a valuable experience, even when I've done it with fellow instructors who had no martial arts background. Though they lacked extensive knowledge, their street experience and understanding of the objective of versatile defensive tactics techniques were most helpful. The weakness in this approach is that if all the instructors have limited knowledge, some solutions may not be found and misinformation might get passed on.

Understanding the versatility of techniques is valuable for instructors and students. Instructors can offer good advice and solutions for the inevitable "what if" questions, and over time they gain a greater understanding of all the nuances that make the techniques work. Students benefit because they learn how to apply just a few techniques to a variety of situations, which results in a more comprehensive understanding of them.

Examine your defensive tactics program to see how your techniques can be applied to a variety of situations. Through exploration, you will find that you can expand your program without having to add one new technique.

REALISTIC TRAINING ENVIRONMENTS

I've been in police work for 29 years, and I have yet to get into a fight on a soft mat or in a wide-open gymnasium. Here are just a few places where I have been in fights with violent people:

- On rooftops
- At the edge of a pier that stretched over a raging river
- On a tiny, second-story porch that had no rails
- In a cramped, flophouse rest room where a urinal and a toilet had been overflowing for several days
- In an upscale restaurant
- On a crowded sidewalk
- In a high school cafeteria
- On the freeway
- Among the rows in a movie theater
- On a crowded bus
- In an elevator
- In the middle of Main Street during rush hour

- In the middle of hundreds of protesters while I was being pummeled with political signs
- In a Vietnam monsoon
- In a biker bar as patrons threw pool balls and pool cues at me
- In the backseat of a car
- In the front seat of a car engulfed in flames

The fact is that most fights happen in cramped, crowded places where there are lots of opportunities to trip over things, run into hard objects, and be attacked by sympathetic friends and relatives of the suspect (I can tell several stories of relatives and best friends jumping my butt as I was making an arrest).

So, if we fight for real in one environment, why do we always train in another?

Any time the training and the real application of what is learned differ, there needs to be a long, hard look at the training. This is one of the primary faults I found with the traditional martial arts systems I studied in my hometown in the mid-1960s, and later while I was serving in the army and stationed in Florida. It's so ridiculous when I look back on it: we would drill for hours on stiff, stylized stepping patterns and stylized blocks, kicks, and punches, but when we sparred or found ourselves in a real fight, we never used them. Instead, we bobbed, weaved, and swatted the attacks aside. Stupidly, I trained this way for several years. Later, when I served as a military policeman in Vietnam, I discovered that my traditional training didn't help me in the many wild and crazy brawls I got into on an almost daily basis working as a military policeman. I decided that when I got home, I would change my way of training.

Here is another example of training and reality not matching. When I joined the Portland Police Bureau in 1972, a large portion of our firearms training consisted of standing sideways to the target, almost at a position of attention, with our nonshooting hand in our pants pocket and our weapon arm extended. It was silly. Who in the hell is going to do that in a gun battle? No one, and I hope there are no police agencies still teaching this absurd position. Hopefully, every agency provides range training that is closer to the realities of what really happens in a hyperventilating, intestine-churning shoot-out.

In the Portland Police Bureau, officers annually practice a variety of realistic driving courses. For example, we practice backing, parking, and maneuvering slowly between cones that represent the same driving conditions that officers experience every day and that account for most fender benders. Then we practice high-speed lane changes, fast cornering, emergency stopping, and ways to control the car in rain-slick and black-ice conditions. As I write this, my agency has begun teaching techniques for driving safely in a pursuit and ways to use speed strips against high-speed eluding cars. Quite a contrast from when I was in the academy back in 1900 and something (yes, there were cars then). At that time we only practiced driving on a straight race track with an occasional slow curve thrown in for variety.

It is beyond my comprehension that while progress is being made to develop realistic training in some areas of police work—such as driving, shooting, high-risk car stops—far too many agencies consistently put their defensive tactics training on the back burner. Fortunately, there are some progressive agencies striving to make their defensive tactics training realistic, but there are lots more stuck in the dark ages when it comes to providing officers with applicable techniques that reflect the ever-increasing dangers in police work.

How Realistic Should You Get?

You should make training as real as you can without getting anyone hurt. Several years ago, I was training in a martial arts school that believed in torturous workouts, including full-contact sparring at medium-to-fast speed. Most of us training were in our 20s then and thought we were invincible, that pain was something experienced only by white belts. Wrong. The half-dozen of us who trained in this fashion were soon suffering from bloody mouths, lumps on every exposed surface, sprained and broken fingers and toes, and ribs that hurt every time we inhaled and exhaled. It didn't take us long to return to our original method of training, which was light-to-medium contact to the body with controlled, light contact to the head. Before I got wise, however, I introduced similar training to the academy defensive tactics class I was teaching. This was in the mid-1970s, a time when I was the only defensive tactics instructor and didn't have to run my ideas past anyone; I just carried out whatever plan my imagination conjured up. Well, this type of rough-and-tumble training didn't last long in the academy either. I had to call an ambulance twice to carry away injured recruits, and we damaged several classroom walls, broke a couple of hanging clocks, and injured a professional stage actor hired to help with the scenarios. One officer still has a deep facial scar from that academy of 23 years ago. This training was too realistic.

Although it's not necessary to train this way, it's important that you are exposed to situations that take you off the gym mats. You don't need elaborate equipment to spice your training with realism, but you do need a good imagination to recreate, as closely as you can, those situations frequently encountered on the street.

Here are some simple ideas that will add a degree of authenticity to your defensive tactics program.

Environmental Training

Since most fights occur in cramped and cluttered places that in no way resemble your training area, and because environment often affects how you apply your techniques, it only makes sense to try to create similar conditions in your training. Of course, you should never try to learn new material in such adverse conditions. New techniques and concepts need to be practiced in a setting where you can concentrate on the mechanics of the movements. But once you can do your control holds and hand-cuffing techniques smoothly, then you should graduate to realistic environmental training.

Here are a few scenarios you should implement into your practice.

Cluttered-Room Training

This is easy to create and will challenge your execution of even the simplest control hold. To prepare your training area, add clutter to the place where you train. You can use gym bags, scattered shoes, mat rolls, barbell plates, basketballs, chairs, even a dead cat if you can get one and can tolerate the smell. The idea is to force you to contend not only with the mechanics of your technique but also with the distractions of a cluttered floor and how it affects your footing as well as the suspect's. Keep in mind that if the suspect trips over something and starts to go down, there is a very good chance you will go down with him. Don't kick things out of the way to apply your techniques. Instead, work around them as if they were immovable objects.

Alleyway Training

This is similar to cluttered-room training except this time, the setting is real. Find a nearby debris-strewn alleyway or a basement hallway cluttered with the sorts of things that always manage to gather in such places. The worse the place, the better for your training.

When you practice your standing and takedown techniques in this very common street environment, it forces you to think about how your movements need to be modified or even if they need to be modified. Say a situation requires that you take down a suspect. What do you do if midway into the technique you realize he is falling toward a stack of milk jugs? In today's sue-happy world, if you hurt the suspect by inadvertently getting his face sliced open, he will own you and your agency and might even end up being your new chief. It's in your best interest to know how to modify your technique and how to quickly switch to another one when the environment requires it. Alleyway training will get you thinking, discussing, and practicing what can be done and not done in an obstructed environment.

Stairs Training

One morning, my partner and I knocked on the door of an apartment in response to a family fight call. We were already a

little cranky about getting the call only five minutes after we had
gone into service at 7:00 a.m. and before our coffee and then
about having to hike up several flights of stairs to get to the den
of marital bliss.

Somehow they managed to hear our knock over their
screams. The door suddenly jerked open, and we were greeted
by a red-faced, beer-gutted drunk. All he managed to blurt out
was "Cops! What the f#@%" before his wife released a mighty
scream and shoved him out the door.

He smashed into my partner, who was standing on the landing. My partner smashed into me, where I stood one step down.
My partner was quick enough to grab the guy (maybe too quick)
because the three of us went tumbling down the stairs in a tan-
gle of arms, legs, and curses.

We managed to dislodge ourselves—then the fight really
began in earnest on a narrow set of stairs. We flailed and tripped
and stumbled and fell. We eventually got control of the fat slob,
but not without much effort and much painful shin, hip, and
elbow banging against hard steps.

We had never trained on stairs, and even if we had, we still
would have had problems since the guy was so combative. But
even a little training would have helped us perform more
smoothly than we did.

Look at all your techniques to determine what changes need
to be made when you are controlling and handcuffing a suspect
standing on the same step, or when you are above him a couple
of steps or two or three below him. See if you can still lock the
guy's elbow when he is lying across several steps with his head
facing downward. Try to determine where you should position
yourself as you handcuff a standing suspect on stairs so narrow
that only one person at a time can stand on a step.

While these are not particularly difficult issues to study, they
do need to be addressed before you suddenly find yourself scuf-
fling on stairs.

Narrow Hallway
Have you tried to do a prone handcuffing maneuver in a nar-

row hallway? Say you talk a suspect down to the floor, but when you tell him to put his arms out to his sides you discover that he can't because the walls are too close. Surprise! This wouldn't have happened if you had practiced your techniques in a hallway setting where the walls are only three feet apart. Your eyes would have been educated to recognize the narrowness, and you would have immediately seen that you couldn't use the prone hand-cuffing position.

Practice your techniques in a narrow hallway and experiment with what techniques you can use, and ones you can't. Should you use a standing handcuff position, or should you go with a kneeling one? Can you swing your baton in the narrow space? Probably not. What alternatives do you have?

Don't think as some officers do: "Well, I'll just figure out what to do when I'm faced with the problem." Hey, you might not have enough time then. Take a few minutes to practice in a narrow hallway and figure out what you are going to do before you have to do it for real.

In a Bus

The Portland Police Bureau trains in a big bus we scrounged from the city fleet. We use the same techniques from our defensive tactics program that we use in other settings, though modified a little to adapt to the crowded seats that face every which way, the chrome poles that extend from the ceiling to the floor, and the riders who always get in the way. We practice extraction techniques using one to three officers, various ways to move a combative person down the aisle without hurting innocent people, and ways to get a person down the narrow steps when there is insufficient room for an officer to walk beside him.

If you can obtain a bus, great. If you can't, set up a couple of rows of chairs to simulate an aisle and crowded seating conditions.

In a Toilet Stall

There is a scummy cafe in the heart of skidrow where I used to get into fights once or twice a week. The fights never happened out in the semiclean eating section, but always in the filthy, cramped rest room and usually in one of the stalls. You haven't been in a fight until you have wrestled in a scum-crusted stall with a wino seated on a toilet, his pants around his ankles, as he sprays wine-laced diarrhea into the overflowing, dirty water. Do you prone the guy out, or do you stand him up? You have to decide quickly because he may have a weapon somewhere on his person.

See how your control holds work in a real rest room stall. You will be surprised at how hard it is to apply those same techniques you have gotten so proficient with on the mat in a real-life stall. The smell alone can be debilitating.

In a Crowd

There are times when you have to take someone into custody on the midway of a crowded carnival, on a busy street corner, in a jammed bar, or in the middle of a rock concert. Ideally, you would move the suspect out of the heart of these crowded places to a quiet location more conducive for handcuffing. But then situations are seldom ideal. For example, sometimes you might have backup officers to help keep the crowd back, sometimes you won't.

Because you probably can't practice downtown on Main Street, you have to approximate crowded conditions in your training area. One simple way to create a crowd is to have the other students mill around you as you search and handcuff your prisoner. Of course, cops being cops, there is great potential here for them to exaggerate the situation and goof off. A little of that is OK, but remember that this is a learning experience.

The crowd should be given clear direction to stand close and move about a little, but not get too carried away and completely interfere with what you are doing. Besides, in a real situation you would probably back off if the crowd got too aggressive. Later, you might consider taking it to that extreme in your training, but the initial exercise is for you to experience searching and handcuffing in the midst of a lot of people.

Consider the mood of the crowd, its proximity to you, the actions of particular individuals, the security of your weapon, and so on. In what way do you need to change your tactics when you are surrounded by unfriendlies or when you have to move your prisoner through a crowd of 100 of his best friends? You need to consider exactly where you are. Can you move your prisoner a short distance to a wall so that people are on only one side of you? Is there a table that you can step behind so you have something between you and the crowd? Should you conduct a thorough search, or just a cursory one for your immediate safety and then a more thorough one when you get your prisoner away from the crowd?

When the Suspect Is Seated

Many techniques that work for you in the standing position will also work when the suspect is seated on a chair, sofa, car seat, theater seat, barstool, floor, or park bench. But you still need to experiment so that you will know which techniques work best.

If you are using a pain compliance technique, you need to figure out how to adjust your grip and body position to ensure that you are applying pain. If you are using a leverage technique, you need to understand that the leverage point may be different when the suspect is seated and lower than you, as opposed to when he is standing next to you.

In addition, it's important to keep in mind that just because a person is seated doesn't mean he can't resist. In fact, he is actually in a strong position to pull you over. Therefore, while you modify your technique, consider adjusting your stance to one that gives you maximum stability and strength.

In the Backseat of the Patrol Car

I've got an inch-long scar on my right thumb where a woman kicked me as she lay in the backseat of my car. No, it wasn't a date gone bad, but a violent prisoner who took advantage of my distraction to slam the hard edge of her high-heeled shoe into my thumb joint. I had just wrestled her into cuffs and then into the backseat of my patrol car, where she screamed like a banshee and kicked at anything within range. I had momentarily rested my hand on the door facing and glanced away for a second when, *kuh-biff!* Instant pain, blood, and scar.

Back in the good ol' days when we could get away with treating a scumbag like a scumbag, a prisoner kicked out the back window of my patrol car while I was driving him to jail. I was seriously pissed, because I had an additional hour of paperwork to do. So I stopped the car, jerked open the door, and kicked the asshole square in the jaw. This accomplished two things: it made him stop kicking my window, and it made me feel a whole heck of a lot better. Can't do that anymore, though.

You need to look at your techniques to see which ones work best to get a prisoner into the backseat. Whether the technique causes pain or is one that affects leverage, it must give clear direction, along with your verbal commands, to direct the suspect into your car.

Actually, you have two considerations when dealing with a suspect and your patrol car: how to get him in it and how to get him out. It can be a challenge to get a suspect to bend at the waist and sit in the backseat if he isn't in the mood. I used to simply smack a resisting prisoner in the groin, which usually worked to double him over, then I would give him a little nudge on the shoulder or head to launch him the rest of the way into the backseat. Can't do that anymore, either. Once when I went to smack a guy in the cookies, I missed and nearly broke my knuckle on his six-inch wide cowboy belt buckle.

If you are stumped as to what techniques to use, I'll give you one at no extra charge. In my agency, we teach officers to back a handcuffed suspect against the door opening and then tell him to sit. If he refuses, the officer hooks one of his hands behind the suspect's neck and, if there are onlookers present, announces loudly to the suspect not to bump his head (see Chapter 6, "How to Create a Witness"). You then tug forward on his neck as you simultaneously thrust the fingers of your other hand into his lower stomach, about two inches below his belt. This causes a jackknife effect, bowing the suspect forward. All it takes then is a nudge against his shoulder, and he takes a seat. Another officer can help by crawling across the backseat from the other side of the car and simultaneously jerking the suspect downward, by pulling on his hips or belt, at the same time you do the neck hook and belly thrust.

This technique comes with just about a 100 percent guarantee. Give it a try and, if needed, combine it with any other techniques from your repertoire. For example, if you have a wrist technique that works like a charm, use it when the second officer does the hip tug. Or you may not want to use this technique at all because you have your own super-duper method that consistently works for you. That's fine, too. What is important is that you practice, using handcuffed classmates and a real, live car.

While it may be difficult for some nonpolice people to believe, there are many prisoners who, once you get them into the backseat, don't want to get out. They scream and kick and spin around on the seat and lunge at you when you open the door. All this is made even more difficult for you to deal with because of the cramped conditions caused by the shield or cage that separates the front seat from the prisoners' area.

Here is a simple technique taught by the Portland Police Bureau that requires two officers. You distract the prisoner by pretending to open, say, the driver's side back door. When the prisoner twists around to kick at you, your partner jerks open the other door, which gives him access to the back of the prisoner's head. Your partner then applies pressure with the fingers of both his hands to the area of the prisoner's jaw where it hinges a couple inches forward of the ears. This causes excruciating pain, making the prisoner scoot toward him in an attempt to get relief. He pulls the prisoner toward the door opening until the prisoner's shoulders and upper back are resting on his bent knee. You then team up with your partner, and the two of you grab the prisoner by the armpits and drag him the rest of the way out.

You can't practice this in the classroom. You have to use a real car.

Learn the mechanics of your techniques on the mat and then experiment with them in real environments. You will not only learn much about the many common but often difficult environments you must work in, you will also benefit from gaining a greater understanding of your techniques.

Now let's look at how to train to get the most out of your techniques in your allotted time.

REPETITION PRACTICE

People in the martial arts are always looking for "the secret" that will make them faster, stronger, more flexible, and a better fighter. Is there a secret that only a few masters know and have kept within their inner circle for hundreds of years? Yes, and the secret is this: *train hard.*

Often when I have said this to students, they have replied, "Hey, that's not a secret, and it's no fun either. And it's not even mystical."

Well, that's true. All too many martial artists want a different secret, one that doesn't involve so much straining and so much sweat. Sorry Charlie, but training hard is the only way to get good. There are no shortcuts, no easy paths, no special meditations.

In a way, the idea of training hard really is a secret, since in this day and age too many people are looking for a quick and easy path to martial arts success. I call them the McDonald's Generation People: drive up to the window and get an instant meal. But not everything can be gotten as easily as that. Some things you've got to work for—like physical skill.

High-Rep Practice

I teach for many private security organizations. Although there are a few security officers who really want the training, most ask for it because they just want a record of it in their files; they don't really care about actually learning anything. These can be tough classes to teach because the students don't want to practice, or if they do try a technique, they do it once then sit back down and say, "OK, I got it," and then wait for the next technique to be taught. For the instructor, this can make a three-hour class seem to last eight. It doesn't do any good to tell them that they need to practice the techniques repetitiously. They figure that just because they can do the movement, they have been trained.

In good martial arts schools, techniques are practiced hundreds, even thousands of times. In some schools, for example, students stand in a stance and rep out hundreds of punches and kicks every training session. Other schools, like mine, camouflage repetitions in a variety of drills. While I prefer my way of doing it because it keeps students interested, entertained, and enthused, what is important is that the movements get performed repetitiously.

Repetition practice works well on the firing range. Every time you fire a box of ammo, you get in 50 reps of gripping, sight alignment, trigger pull, and so on. When you spend an afternoon at the range, you may do hundreds of reps; spend a week at the range and you knock off thousands. In time, the movements become ingrained and second nature, which is exactly what you want them to be when the poop hits the fan and you have to shoot fast, without conscious thought. Repetitious practice in defensive tactics will give you the same benefits.

Without a doubt, rep practice is the primary element ("the secret, Grasshopper") that is missing from most defensive tactics programs. There are several reasons for this.

- Instructors don't realize its importance.
- Instructors don't know how to design repetitious practice.
- Police students don't realize its importance.
- Police students are reluctant to do it.
- Time constraints (translation: budget constraints) work against it.

Instructors Don't Realize Its Importance

Students will never be exposed to the benefits of high-rep practice if instructors are unaware of its value. The most common reason many instructors are unaware is because they are the product of some two-day instructor workshop, where at the end of the second day—*poof!* You're a defensive tactics instructor. And who is it poofing them? Usually another officer who got poofed a couple years earlier. The value of rep practice was never learned, and therefore it was never passed on.

The only time I can recall seeing an instructor drill a police defensive tactics class repetitiously was when the instructor also practiced a martial art outside of the police job. This instructor would never even consider letting his defensive tactics class practice a wristlock only three or four times and then move on to something else. His police students practiced as if they were in a martial arts school, performing one technique dozens of times, sometimes at their own pace, sometimes to the instructor's count. In the end, these police students had a deep understanding of their techniques, and they looked great doing them.

Instructors Don't Know How to Design Repetitious Practice

We are going to get into this more in a moment, but for now let's just say that many instructors think of repetitious practice, if they think of it at all, as simply telling their class: "OK, everybody, now practice that four or five times." There is more to it than that, as we will soon see.

Police Students Don't Realize Its Importance

If you are an instructor, there is no excuse for you not knowing the value of rep practice and other drills that enhance learning. It's your job to know it. If you choose to take on the responsibility of being an instructor, then you also assume the responsibility of learning all you can about the subject and how to teach it. You should read books and magazine articles, study videos, and take classes from other instructors.

Students, however, are just, well, students. They don't know anything about, or they have a limited knowledge of, the subject. They just do whatever and believe whatever they are told, assuming or hoping that the instructor knows what the hell he is talking about (an instructor friend of mine says this about students: "If they are dumb enough to ask, tell them anything"). So if the student has never been exposed to the concept of rep practice, he will never know what he is missing.

If you are a student, do you have a responsibility to search out additional information on the subject of defensive tactics, which would increase your chance of learning about rep practice?

Of course. Every officer should learn as much as he can about his job, especially those things that relate to survival. The problem is that if the officer is fat, dumb, and happy, believing the defensive tactics he learned are all that he needs, it would never occur to him to search further.

I hope that is not you. If there is any doubt about your training, any part that was unsatisfactory, then you should make the effort and seek out more information.

Police Students Don't Like to Train Hard

In all the years I have taught defensive tactics, I can recall only a small minority of officers, new and veteran alike, who liked to practice repetitions. Talk about grumbling. "This hurts." "I'm tired." "I have a bad shoulder." "OK, I got it," they say after three reps. "Now what are we going to do?"

My reply? "No, you don't have it." "So what if it hurts? We're not playing checkers." "You're supposed to get tired." "If you have a bad shoulder, let's figure a way to work around it."

If you are reluctant to train hard, realize this *fact:* the only way you are going to develop any degree of skill in defensive tactics is to practice repetitiously. Doing a wristlock three times will do absolutely nothing for you, and the chance of your executing the technique under the stress of a real situation is about the same as Madonna getting into a convent.

Will you be able to perform the movement the next day in class without a refresher? Maybe, maybe not. That depends on your retention ability for this kind of material. But whether you can do the technique in class again without help doesn't really prove anything, anyway. The real test is whether you can do the intricacies of a technique under stress after having practiced it only three times. I say you can't.

You must practice a movement so many times that it becomes ingrained in your conscious and subconscious mind. How many times? I don't know; it's different for everyone. That's like asking a range officer how long before you score a 95? Who knows? Each officer is different. For you to master a defensive tactics movement might take 500 repetitions spread over two weeks, while for me it might take 1,000 reps spread over six weeks, since I'm sort of a slow learner.

You will know when you have arrived, because the technique will suddenly become second nature to you. You will be able to do it as you talk to a third person, and you will be able to do it effortlessly even while someone screams in your face. The technique will become part of your conscious and subconscious mind, making it seem as if your muscles have their own memory. Will you be at this level after three reps? No way. One thousand? Maybe.

Time Contraints

Time is a big issue that is usually tied directly to an agency's budget, which means that defensive tactics training often gets reduced because of limited money allotted to training. It's been my experience that when there is a money crunch, the brass is quick to cut defensive tactics training, though they never touch those classes that are politically correct, such as "Cultural Diversity" and "How to Be Nice to a Wino." While these classes are important (bullshitbullshitbullshit), they aren't going to do you much good when a gargantuan outlaw biker with muscles and veins in his forehead is slapping your face with a manhole cover.

If you are the instructor, what do you do? Well, you do the best you can with the time you do have.

First, look at your program to see if there are ways to save time, such as the following:

- Reduce war stories—yours and students'.
- Eliminate warm-up time when the training that follows doesn't warrant it.
- Eliminate talking among students—when they are talking they are not doing reps.
- Reduce free practice since it's usually less productive than when the instructor counts reps.
- Reduce break times or eliminate them. Allow students to use the rest room as needed.
- Make explanations efficient—many instructors tend to

overexplain a technique (I'm guilty). Say what you've got to say and then shut up.

- Volunteer to spend a few minutes of your lunchtime with slow learners—those students who have two left feet (you know, the way you used to be).
- Control the class clowns—cops love to goof off and have a laugh. But when time is limited, nip that behavior quickly.

There are lots of other time wasters, but you get the idea. It's amazing how much more you can get done when you start trimming the fat.

TIME-SAVING WAYS TO PRACTICE REPS

There is an old saying in the martial arts: "It's better to do 10 correct repetitions than 100 poor ones." I disagree. I tell my students that it's better to do 500 correct ones than 100 poor ones. I have always believed in the value of high-rep practice and have written about it in my other martial arts books *Speed Training, Power Fighting*, and *The Way Alone* (also available from Paladin Press). In the last book, I tell how I used rep training to prepare for my second-degree black belt test in 1972 when my training time was restricted. In a nutshell, here is how I did it.

I was stuck in the police academy for 18 weeks, unable to get to my karate school to train. So, I would go into my small spare bedroom at home, which was empty, and write down on a piece of paper how many reps I was going to do that day, such as 500 punches, 100 backfists, 1,000 front kicks, 600 roundhouse kicks. Sometimes my pen was more enthusiastic than my body, and I would realize 20 minutes into my workout that I had written down numbers far too large for how I felt that day. No matter. That was what I put down so that is what I had to do (sometimes discipline can be a terrible thing). I recall several training sessions when I literally crawled out of the room, my legs too weak to support me.

It paid off though. I passed the test a month after I got out of the academy, and boy was I sharp. Although that kind of training would kill me today, I learned from those grueling months that the secret to success in the martial arts is to do volumes of repetitions. I believe there are two elements to repetition practice that should exist in any given training session: the exercise should be productive, and it should be interesting. If an exercise isn't productive and helping you learn, then toss it out and get one that does. If the drill isn't interesting, you are going to lose your concentration, which means an unproductive training experience.

As mentioned earlier, I believe in "hiding" repetitions in my drills. When I began karate training in 1965, we spent countless hours sitting in "horse" stance (a squatting, bowed leg position as if you were riding a fat horse) punching the air. I probably threw three, maybe four ka-zillion punches (no exaggeration) those first two years. The training was grueling because that was how it was done in the Orient. Since I was cursed with discipline, I always did it and always came back for more, while all of the other original students eventually dropped out. Since we weren't in the Orient and not of that culture, the others just couldn't relate to why we should accept the pain and the monotony—and have to pay monthly dues for it. I, on the other hand, loved it.

Martial arts have been in this country for 40 years now, and the fighting arts and training concepts have evolved dramatically. There are new and improved ways to do things, ways that can be enormously fun and that result in better students. It's been my experience that the more fun and interesting the training is, the more productive it's going to be. You can accomplish this by developing a variety of training drills that mask the fact that you are practicing repetitiously.

Here are a few I use to hide repetitions. My students always find them fun and, as a result, productive.

Breaking Down Techniques

I used to compete in the kata division back in my karate competition days. Kata is like a floor exercise in gymnastics, except with kata you are simulating a fight between you and a half-dozen attackers. Some katas are hundreds of years old, while others have been developed by modern-day masters (check out American Kata, available through my web page: http://www.aracnet.com/~lwc123/). We have four in my style, all of which have 100 moves and take about two and a half minutes to do. A panel of judges rates competitors on speed, power, precision of movement, balance, degree of difficulty, mental attitude, and warrior spirit.

Most karate practitioners practice their kata from beginning to end. I discovered, however, that I benefited more when I broke the kata down into individual techniques. I would do the first move say, 10 times, then the second move 10 times, and so on. When I felt comfortable with my performance of each individual move, I would combine two moves and do them 10 times. Then I would combine three moves, then four moves, then five, proceeding through the entire kata. As competition day neared, I would break the kata into four parts and do the first 25 moves 10 times, the second 25 moves 10 times, and so on. Then I would practice the first half of it 10 times and then the second half 10 times. Not until three or four days before the competition would I do the kata in its entirety.

I didn't always practice my kata in sequential order. Some days I would practice the last few moves first, if I felt those needed extra work. Sometimes I would do more reps of some techniques than I would of others. If I felt the first half of the form was looking sharp, I would only do five reps of it, but do 10 or more reps of the second half.

This approach helped me win or place in more than 50 tournaments, capturing overall grand champion in a few and getting rated three times in the Top Ten in *Karate Illustrated* magazine. Am I cool? Yes, just ask my dog. The point I'm making, however, is that by breaking down the moves, I could concentrate better, correct problems, and obtain a better understanding of the techniques.

Will this work for police defensive tactics? Yup. Let's look at a simple defense against a shove and see how you can break it down into sections and then practice them with high reps.

Stand facing your partner as if interviewing him on the street.

As he reaches forward with his right hand to shove you, swat it aside in the direction of his other arm, step in toward his right side and grab his right upper arm with your left hand and his right wrist with your right hand. You are now standing at his side, holding his arm in what is sometimes called "the minimum custody hold," a position commonly used to walk a nonviolent subject, or a point from which, if he insists on being aggressive, you can execute a number of pain compliance holds and takedowns. Let's break this simple defense move into four parts.

1. *Training the eye.* Students should form two lines and face each other. On the instructor's count, the students forming line A will attack their partners in line B by thrusting their hands forward as if to push. Line B will only watch the thrust. This drill is to let each student observe how his partner looks as he executes the thrust: how his shoulders move, how his hand moves forward, where his eyes look, and how he moves his feet. At this point, the drill is to educate the eye to recognize those movements, subtle and not so subtle, that initiate a push. This knowledge will help students react more quickly because they have learned to recognize the signals. Both lines should do 20 reps with each hand.

2. *The block.* When the instructor counts aloud during this phase, line A will thrust their hands forward to do the push, and line B, who are standing in an interview position with their left side angled forward, will swat the attack aside with their left hand. The swat should be short and quick, with no extension or wasted motion. Each line will do 20 reps from both the left and right side.

3. *Two-handed grab.* As the instructor counts, line A will push, and line B will swat the hand away as before and then step in slightly with their lead foot and grab the attacker's upper arm with their left hand and the attacker's wrist with their right. Students in line B will freeze in place at this point, though they still need to complete their step. Each line will do 20 reps with the left side and right side forward.

4. *Completing the movement on the count.* Line A pushes while

line B blocks, steps forward, and grabs the attacker's arm as before. Line B then steps the rest of the way in and turns in the same direction as the attacker is facing. Line B can now escort the attacker in a forward direction or execute any number of other moves (personally, if someone tried to push me, I would dump the asshole on his back, but then that's just me). Each line does 20 reps with the left side and right side forward.

This four-part exercise gives you 80 reps with each arm for a total of 160 reps. When you consider that the attacker is also getting to watch his partner practice 160 moves, both of you benefit from 320 repetitions. Not bad for an exercise that will take no longer than 15 minutes for both lines to complete. It's highly productive, and because the exercise is broken into multiple parts, it holds your interest because there is always a new phase to work.

During the next practice section, the instructor can drill the students on the entire movement or, if he feels extra practice on a particular phase is needed, he can again break the movement into four parts.

Monkey Line

This is another of my favorites that provides practice against a variety of opponents. I will discuss this in detail later.

Line Drill

The line drill is a universal way to train that has survived the test of time because of its versatility and the fact that it's so beneficial. Students form two lines facing each other. When the room is too small for the number of students, I position them diagonally toward opposite corners. Sometimes I've had so many people in a class that I have had to use two sets of lines. If you have this many students and they are untrained, you definitely need more than one instructor.

For the instructor, one advantage of the line drill is that it allows him to look down the rows and easily see students who are making errors. He can stand at one end and look at as many as 40 people and easily spot a student who is out of sync with the others. He can then go to the problem and get it taken care of.

The line drill also provides students with a variety of training partners. At the completion of one set of exercises, the instructor can call for everyone to move to the right to the next partner. The end students step over to the opposite line and become part of it.

The variety of exercises that can be done in the line drill is up to the instructor's imagination. I select drills limited in movement so that the integrity of the line doesn't collapse. For example, a drill where line A steps over and applies a wristlock on line B is easier to control than one where two dozen partners are moving around in a clinch, leg sweeping and proning each other out all over the floor.

Students like the structure of the line drill because it's beneficial, versatile, and fun to practice reps to the instructor's cadence. Instructors like it because it keeps the class orderly, it's a good way to handle numerous people, and it's easy to see those students who are having problems.

Pantomiming

Martial arts students don't have a problem with pantomiming because they do it so often in their training. I have found that police officers, however, are self-conscious doing it. As the name implies, pantomiming involves students practicing a given movement in the air without a partner. If they are drilling on responding to the suspect's push we just discussed, they would pantomime it by swatting the air to block the imaginary shove, stepping forward, and then simulating the hand movements involved in grabbing the arm and applying a wristlock.

If the instructor can get police officers past the self-conscious phase (this can be done by introducing pantomiming exercises in the recruit academy), they will find it to be a beneficial supplement to other ways of practice. It's so easy that it can be done before, during, and after class; during lunch breaks; and at home.

When pantomiming a motion, it's important to do the movement exactly as it would be done on a live person. Use your imagination to see and feel the person you are doing the technique on. Don't shortcut movements by moving your body or arm insufficiently. It's better to exaggerate the movements than to reduce what would be necessary to really execute the technique.

Uchikomi

I wrote a chapter on *uchikomi* (a Japanese word meaning "to enter") in my book *Speed Training* and discussed how judo and jujitsu people use it to develop speed and form. Uchikomi is similar to practicing partial reps, though I think of partials as being done at slow to medium speed to improve the execution and the understanding of a technique. Uchikomi should be practiced after you are familiar with a technique and at a point where you want to add speed and smoothness to the "opening" move.

The opening move, or the entering phase of a technique, can be hazardous to your health if you don't do it right. Any time you have to cross the gap from an outside range, where you are relatively safe, to an inside range, where it's going to be hands-on time, you run the risk of getting punched in the snot box. Uchikomi is a good way to concentrate only on the elements of crossing the gap.

Let's say you are going to practice a handcuffing technique where you cuff the suspect's hands behind his back. You begin by reaching out with your right hand and grabbing your training partner's upper left arm as you step across the gap. The palm of your left hand covers the back of his hand, and you carry it to the small of his back where you apply a painful wrist flex. From here you order him to put his other hand on the back of his head and spread his feet and then you apply the handcuffs. To practice uchikomi, you only do the reach, step, hand cover, and wrist flex, and not do the handcuffing phase.

This drill can be done using the monkey line, the line drill, pantomiming, or any other exercise you can dream up. Using the line drill, for example, the instructor would have two lines of students face each other. On the count, line A would step quick-

To practice uchikomi when practicing handcuffing, the officer only executes the first three steps, the entry phase. He grabs the suspect's upper arm and reaches for his hand. He scoops the suspect's hand and begins moving it behind him.

ly across the gap, grab their partners' upper arm, scoop their hand, and move it quickly to their partners' lower back. The move is completed when the student acting as the officer feels that he is in a strong position to cuff. But instead of cuffing, he will step back and repeat the move again on the instructor's count. Each line should do 10 to 20 reps.

Look at the entering phase of all of your techniques and see how you can practice uchikomi. This is an especially good way to practice when a class has lots of injuries from past sessions that need to heal, when you can't get mats for the day, or when you just want to practice that all-important phase of closing the gap.

Visualization

I've written a lot about visualization for magazines and in several of my books available through Paladin Press, most recently, *Deadly Force Encounters*. Yes, that was a plug, but I also wanted to make the point that I think the concept of visualization is an important one. It's used by high-speed shooters on the U.S. Special Operations Command, by Britain's Special Air Service, by many gunfight survivors, and by top competitive shooters.

Many of these experts may not call what they do *visualiza-tion* out of concern that the term may sound too esoteric. But whether it's called visualization, mental imagery, or "running through it in my head," it's a form of sweatless practice that you can do while sprawled on your sofa or lying in a hammock under a tree. It works best when you are in a quiet place and deeply relaxed, though to a lesser degree you can still benefit by doing it whenever and wherever you can. You don't need to chant any-thing, burn incense, or kill a lamb. All you need to bring to the task is your natural ability to make pictures in your mind of a given event. You do it all the time now. You make mental pic-tures when you try to recall where you left something and dur-ing those times at home when you are thinking about a particu-larly dangerous call you had that day. In *Deadly Force Encounters*, I talk about ways to visualize entire shooting scenarios while sit-ting in the parking lot of a 7-11 or while having coffee in a diner.

A friend of mine, a top-ranked competitive shooter, visual-izes shooting people while he rides the bus to work. He likes to pick out one of those purple-haired freaks, you know, the one with rings piercing his lips and eyebrows, who sprawls in the back of the bus with his Doc Marten boots in the aisle. While the freak bobs his head to some heavy metal music blaring from his headphones, my friend calmly sits at the front of the bus and visualizes double-tapping rounds into his forehead. He sees clearly in his mind's eye the front sight of his weapon with ol' purple hair boy's face just beyond it. He mentally lines up his sights, squeezes his trigger, and releases two rounds.

Is such practice sick? Some people might think so, especially those who live relatively soft lives, never having to face the drag-on every day as cops do. But as a police officer, my friend may have to shoot a real human being, and if it happens, he will go into it knowing he has trained shooting paper targets at the range and mentally shooting people on his bus.

Let's take a quick look at how you can use visualization in your defensive tactics training. Let's say you want to mentally practice freeing the hand of a motorist who is refusing to let go of his steering wheel. Begin by seeing yourself standing to the rear of the door opening and looking in at the seated driver, who is white-knuckling his steering wheel. See yourself lift your left hand to the left side of your face for protection as you lightly smack the side of the driver's face with your right hand. Then see yourself reach down with your right hand, pry his thumb from the steering wheel, pull his arm back, and apply a wrist technique. Be sure that you feel the suspect's face, hand, and arm in your mind. This imaginary feeling is called kinesthetics, and it's an important aspect of the visualization process.

When you mentally practice any kind of defensive tactic, be aware of your mental picture to ensure that it's as clear and realistic as you can make it. Your imagined scene should be brightly lit and in color. Imagine the suspect standing in different places, such as to your front, right, left, or rear, and see and feel yourself turn to face him. If you want the imagined suspect to resist, see in your mind how fast he is resisting. Is he just stiffening his arm to your imagined grab, or is he flailing it around? Fill the scene with objects, such as cars jammed into a high-rise parking structure, furniture in a cramped living room, or clutter in a warehouse.

If you were really doing the technique, it would take about 10 seconds to execute, which is exactly how long it should take you to visualize it. Always visualize at the same speed at which it would take you to do the activity for real. At this rate, you can visualize about five reps of dealing with the stubborn motorist each minute. That's 25 reps in five minutes. Visualize this just three days a week and you will get in 75 reps. Pretty cool, huh? And you do them all from the comfort of your chair.

Let's now look at a technique that most officers need extra work on. With most handcuffing techniques that use pain compliance to control the suspect while applying the handcuff, the first cuff generally goes on smoothly while the second cuff is more difficult to manipulate. Let's get some extra reps in and visualize putting on that second cuff.

Whether you are visualizing the standing or the prone position, begin your imagery with the first cuff already on and then proceed with mentally putting on the second one. Make your suspect wear long sleeves so that you have to deal with getting them out of the way. Give him a broad back and short arms so that you really have to struggle to get the cuffs on. Make his shoulders stiff. Remember to visualize the process at the same speed that it would take if you were really applying the second cuff. Do three a minute for five minutes and you will knock out 15 to 20 reps.

Many officers are hurt when interviewing a suspect who suddenly throws a surprise their way. It only takes a split second for the situation to turn and, if you are not prepared, your reaction will be poor to nonexistent. You can reduce the element of surprise in this situation by visualizing all the possibilities that can happen and your reaction to them. This is not as overwhelming as it may seem because the suspect can only do a few actions. He can punch or kick, turn and run, or dive for a nearby weapon. Even though there are variations of these three actions, visualization will definitely help you react more smoothly no matter how you do it.

Begin by visualizing yourself standing about three feet away from the suspect in your usual interview stance. See him suddenly lunge toward you with both arms extended as if to give you a shove. See yourself sidestep quickly, knock his arms away, step back, and draw your baton. Visualize this about 20 times for five minutes and then move on to another scenario. This time, the suspect lunges for a beer bottle that is on a nearby table. See yourself . . . well, you get the idea.

The beauty of this is that if a situation goes down similar to what you have visualized, you will react as if you had practiced a response, which you had, though only in your mind. Even if the real attack isn't the same as you visualized, your reaction will nonetheless be far more polished than if you had not practiced visualization at all.

Research shows that three to five minutes of visualization is sufficient to make improvement. It's difficult for most people to concentrate for much longer than that, and if your mind wanders too much, you lose the benefit of the exercise. Of course, you can have as many sessions as you want throughout the day, because as with most practice, the more you do it the better you get. Visualization works. Try it.

Whether you are practicing karate, jujitsu, or police defensive tactics, rep practice is the secret to success in the fighting arts. Restricted training time is a problem in many agencies, so much so that training often consists of the instructor demonstrating a technique, the students practicing it once or twice, and then the instructor moving on to something else. No matter how little time an agency provides for defensive tactics training, it's important for the training staff to look for ways to incorporate rep training. In fact, rep training becomes more significant the less time you have to train, because it makes training time more efficient.

On a physical level, I think of rep training as sanding a block of wood. When you first learned how to apply handcuffs on a suspect, it was as if you were given a rough piece of wood to sand. Every time you practiced putting the cuffs on, you made a couple of swipes on the wood with sandpaper. In time, your practice rubbed the wood smooth of all the bumps and knots. On a mental level, repetitious practice dramatically imprints a technique in your mind. The more reps you do, the deeper the imprint and the longer it stays in the ol' gray matter. In time, the imprint will be permanently entrenched and become a part of your repertoire that will be there for you in stressful situations.

I cannot stress enough the value of high-repetition training.

WHAT THE HECK IS *TOKUIWAZA?*

In judo there is a term, *tokuiwaza*, that describes techniques personalized to suit the specific judo player who developed them. Usually it means that one or more techniques have been altered to fit the build and body of a specific player; often it becomes that person's signature technique. Muhammad Ali's quick jab is one example, and Bruce Lee's extraordinary backfist is another. My purpose in mentioning tokuiwaza here is that all too often there is an expectation in police defensive tactics programs that there is only one way to execute a technique.

Instructors take the approach that this is how it's done, and every officer will do it this way.

This is wrong.

A Couple of Examples

I once had a police officer in my martial arts school who studied with me for about three years. From his first day, he favored a high fighting stance, standing virtually straight up to his full 6 feet. I tried in vain to get him to bend his legs and lower himself into a crouch as he worked the drills and sparred with the other students. He tried, but a minute or two later he would be standing straight up again.

After about a year of constant badgering, I began to notice something that surprised me: his high stance was working for him. In fact, he had earned a couple of belts and was becoming quite skilled. So I quit riding him about his high stance, and he went on to earn two degrees of brown belt and become one of my senior students. What made me realize that he had achieved tokuiwaza was the night he blasted me in the mouth with a punch that left four of my bottom teeth protruding through my lower lip.

In another instance in the early 1970s, I was teaching a police academy defensive tactics class in which there was a young female named Sue, who stretched the tape to 5 feet, 4 inches and weighed maybe 115 pounds. One day I was teaching carotid constraint holds, showing various ways of getting behind the suspect, how to wrap the arm around his neck, and the best way to take him to the ground where he would drift off into sleepy land. Although the average person can easily learn and execute the classic carotid constraint holds, three students in the class were complaining that their opponents were too tall to do the techniques exactly the way I taught them. A fourth student, Sue, realized that as the smallest person in the class, she could not even begin to do the techniques using the methods I had shown, but she didn't whine about it like the others. Instead, she ran across the floor and up behind the tallest person in class, a 6-foot, 5-inch mountain of a guy. As if she were climbing stairs, she grabbed him by his shoulders and placed her right foot behind his knee, her left foot behind his thigh, and then her right on his hip, and climbed up his back until she could wrap her arm around his neck and ride him like a cowgirl on a horse.

Now, I don't recommend this approach as an alternative to other variations of applying a carotid constraint. My point is that she was astute enough to recognize that what I was showing wouldn't work for her, and that she needed to come up with something that would. (Sue went on to be an outstanding uniformed officer, a renowned homicide investigator, and an advisor on a television police show. She died in 1996, when TWA flight 800 exploded mysteriously over the Eastern Coast, killing everyone on board.)

Unfortunately, such innovativeness doesn't happen often enough, and I place the blame for this on the instructors and their defensive tactics programs. I have often seen instructors look blank when asked by a student why a technique wasn't working for him. The instructor didn't have a solution because all he knew were the rudiments of the basic technique. He knew how to teach it to work, but he didn't know what to do when it didn't. Unfortunately, not all students are as perceptive and innovative as Sue was; they don't always see the solutions and are therefore left with techniques that are useless to them.

Let's look at a typical situation that will affect the execution of a standard defensive tactics technique.

When the Officer Is Taller or Shorter Than the Suspect

Consider the bent-arm wristlock, a technique where you stand side by side with the suspect and bend his arm until his forearm is vertical and his elbow is braced against your stomach. You apply downward pressure against the back of the suspect's hand, which locks his wrist joint and results in extreme pain.

It's a good technique that has been used by police agencies forever, but works best when the giver and the receiver are close in height. When there is a great height discrepancy, it can be awkward, if not impossible, to do the standard way. This is where common sense among instructors often flies out the window. Far too many fail to acknowledge this problem, which means that the very tall or very short student is left with a void in his training. To give these students a workable technique, the instructor needs to personalize the movement so it works for everyone. The problem is that too many instructors know only how to teach a technique one way.

If that is the case in your agency and you are having problems with a technique, you need to take it upon yourself to seek out a solution. If there are officers in your agency experienced in martial arts, especially the grappling arts, ask their advice. Go to a judo or jujitsu school and explain to the instructor what you need. Consider taking a few private lessons to learn other ways to apply the technique to make it work in all situations.

Physical force situations are seldom ideal. I am 5 feet, 11 inches, which isn't considered extremely tall, nor is it considered short. Nonetheless, I have had to drastically modify my regular defensive tactics techniques often because of extreme height differences between me and suspects I have arrested.

Tokuiwaza—personalizing your techniques by modifying them—is something you should know how to do even if your height is in the average range. You will always be running into people vertically cursed in one direction or the other. So not only is it a good idea to know variations, but the process of learning them will greatly increase the understanding of all your techniques.

KUZUSHI

Here is another Japanese word: *kuzushi*. No, it's not something you say after someone sneezes, that's *gesundheit*, which is German. Kuzushi, pronounced koo-zoo-she, means the state of being unbalanced, and it's found in the fighting arts of judo and jujitsu. It's also called the point of unbalance, a place where a person's body is slightly or greatly unstable. Let me explain how I think of kuzushi. While my approach may or may not be the way that it's taught in formal jujitsu schools, it works for me and my students.

Because my training partner's kuzushi is leaning back, it's easy for me to push him down to the floor using only my finger.

Tripod Theory

To stay upright, we should all be built like a tripod, but we are able to stand on only two legs because we all have equilibrium, something that exists within our heads and continually works to keep us from falling over in a heap. In spite of the miracle of equilibrium, our balance is nonetheless weak in the direction where that third leg would be if we were a tripod. For example, if you stood straight with your feet about 18 inches apart, your third leg would have to be centered in front of you, roughly 12 to 15 inches out, or centered behind you, 12 to 15 inches.

If someone were to push against your left shoulder from your side, your ability to resist would be strong because you are stabilized by your right leg. But if you were pushed against the center of your chest in the direction of where your third leg would be, you would stagger backward. Or, if you were pushed between your shoulder blades in the direction of where the third leg would be to the front, you would stagger forward.

It doesn't require great force to upset a person's balance because his upper body is weak at only one inch off vertical. I like to explain kuzushi to a class by having a student stand up and then lean back an inch or two. I then use my index finger to push downward at the top of his chest, just below the hollow of his throat. It's fun to watch the class react as my demonstrator plops onto his back at my feet.

Of course, you can also use greater force to take advantage of a person's kuzushi. One time I came out of a restaurant to find a guy urinating against the side of my police car. In a burst of temper and a rush of speed, I charged like a berserk water buffalo and rammed my shoulder against the pisser's upper torso. My energy exploded through his body in the direction of his third leg (the invisible support one, not the one peeing all over the door of my police car), which sent the guy hurdling across the sidewalk, asshole over teakettle. Not only did he get some serious abrasions all over his body, he was soaked with pee pee, too.

I'll talk more about the tripod theory in a moment and show you how you can use it to your advantage, and how it can be used against you.

Eight Directions of Unbalance

Jujitsu practitioners take advantage of eight directions in which their opponent's balance can be upset. Those directions are forward, backward, right, left, diagonal forward left, diagonal forward right, diagonal backward left, and diagonal backward right. Think of it this way: a person standing upright with his feet planted firmly and arms hanging straight down is in a balanced position, but when he leans in any one of the eight directions, his balance becomes weak, making him vulnerable.

There are two ways a suspect can become unbalanced: inadvertently or by being forced into it by a big, mean police officer like you.

Taking Advantage of Someone's Kuzushi

This is the easiest because the person does all the work for you. All you have to do is recognize the moment and take advantage of it. Let's look at a situation where a big, fat jerk tried to push me.

The vice president of the United States was in town giving a speech at our convention center. Outside, the purple-haired freaks and the great unwashed were protesting his visit with shouts, sign waving, and the occasionally tossed tomato. When their lawful protest turned into a frenzy, we moved in to arrest the primary agitators.

I was on one of several arrest teams, a squad of officers who would move into the ugly crowd and surround a targeted person. While eight officers formed into a circle and faced outward to watch the crowd, two other officers would handcuff the agitator. Then the eight officers would escort the two officers with the prisoner out of the crowd and off to a waiting bus.

One time, I was one of the eight surrounding an arrest. As we were moving out of the crowd, a big, fat, long-haired creep tried to block my way with his body. When he saw that I wasn't going to stop or move, he reached out to push me. By reaching toward me, he placed himself in one of the eight directions of unbalance. "Thank you very much, you dumb shit," I said to myself.

I quickly and cleverly sidestepped, reached up for a handful of his greasy hair, and jerked him forward and down in the direction of his kuzushi. Though the guy outweighed me by 30 pounds, it didn't matter because his kuzushi made him weak. His face went into the pavement like a man starving for an asphalt lunch. It was so cool I impressed myself.

People seldom stand in a straight-up, perfectly balanced stance, with their feet directly under them. Most of the time they lean in one of the eight directions with their feet positioned in any number of ways. People slump forward, lean back, stretch, cross their feet, brace themselves against a wall, bend to straighten their socks, lean back to scratch behind their knee, and so on. These positions and dozens like them place people in a position of unbalance.

When a subject resists your arrest, he doesn't do it by standing straight up with his feet evenly spaced beneath him. He pushes, pulls, leans this way and that, and while sometimes he is greatly unbalanced and other times he is only slightly unbalanced, it doesn't matter because once he gives up his balance, his butt is yours; he is handing it to you on a silver platter and doesn't even know it. But you know it, because you wisely bought this book and learned how to recognize and take advantage of it.

The Clinch

You grab the drunken motorist, and the fight is on. Most often the fight quickly takes the form of a clinch, your hands gripping his arms, and his hands gripping yours. Or one or both of you grab a shoulder and a shirt front and then jostle and waltz about with each other. Judo and jujitsu practitioners spar from this position and call it *randori*.

When your partner pulls down on your left arm, his kuzushi has to go to the right. When he pushes against your right shoulder, his kuzushi extends diagonally to his left. Every time he pushes or pulls you, he is slightly or greatly off balance in one of the eight directions. When this happens, you want to yield in whatever direction his balance extends and then add a technique to continue his energy moving in that direction. I like to practice with my eyes closed, which increases my sensitivity to my partner's unbalanced weight.

It's easy to catch people off balance who are not trained in the grappling arts. But against people who understand kuzushi, it's considerably harder. A couple years ago I felt good, almost cocky, about my ability to react to an opponent's kuzushi. I could easily respond to untrained cops in the academy and karate people who had limited or no grappling experience. However, one day I was training with a muscular, second-degree black belt in jujitsu and discovered, to my chagrin, that I couldn't budge the guy. Each time I felt him begin to lean in one of the eight directions, I would try to force him to overextend so I could dump him. Forget about it. The guy was solid as a building—heck, make that a high-rise building. He knew what I was doing and would quickly regain his balance and then take advantage of my energy extension and dump my cuteness on the mat.

Recognizing a Kuzushi Opportunity on the Street

I've listed below five out of hundreds of typical street situations where you can take advantage of a suspect's kuzushi. To make it easy for you, I've italicized the places where the suspect is off balance. Visualize them in your mind and imagine what you would do.

- Just as you walk up to the driver's door, the motorist, armed with a large wrench, pushes open his door, *leans out and twists his body back to face you.*

From the clinch, when my partner pulls down on my left arm, I add to his unbalanced position by pushing up on his left elbow with my right hand. From here, I could easily spin him down to the floor.

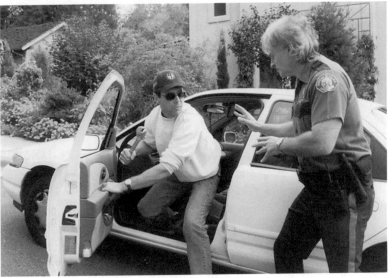

As the motorist exits his car armed with a wrench, he is leaning forward and supporting himself on one leg. The officer could easily pull him to the pavement and onto his face.

- As you approach the unwanted in the tavern, he slides off his stool and *quickly reaches down to pick up the stool next to him.*
- Angry that you stopped him, the outlaw biker pulls off his Nazi helmet, grips it like a club, and *swings his leg over his motorcycle.*
- Just as you grab the suspect's upper arm, *he leans forward to pull away from your grasp.*
- You approach the drunken woman from behind and grab her upper arms. *She bends forward in a twisting motion.*

How to Create Kuzushi

Forcing a person into a position of kuzushi is easy, except when trying to do it against an experienced jujitsu practitioner, as I mentioned earlier. You can do it with a nudge, shove, pull, trip, fake, kick, punch, slap, or even with words. Here are some examples.

From Behind

Say you are talking to an angry motorist who has been stopped because he is suspected of driving under the influence. The suspect is standing outside his car, and just as you tell him you want to see him do a couple of field sobriety tests, he turns and moves to get back in his car. As he places his right leg in, you press the bottom of your foot into the back of his left leg (depending on the situation you can make this a hard thrusting kick or just an easy press). The idea is to bend his support leg so that it begins to collapse, which will cause him to lean backward in one of the eight directions of unbalance.

You now grab him by his shoulder or collar and jerk him back and down, or you can reach around and place your palm against his forehead and pull him back as you push against the small of his back with your other hand. Your objective is to get him onto his back or on his butt and then maneuver him into a position to be handcuffed.

A woman resists by leaning her balance forward. A foot sweep could easily send her to the sidewalk.

As a suspected drunken driver leans back to get into his car, the officer pulls down on the motorist's shoulders and presses his foot behind his knee to buckle his leg.

From the Side

You are standing side by side with a subject as you hold him in the minimum custody position, your left hand on his upper arm, your right hand on his wrist. He doesn't like it and steps toward you to knock you off balance. Big mistake for Mr. Caca Breath. You yield to his push and shuffle-step to the side. You then pull his wrist in a downward direction as you simultaneously grab a handful of his hair at the back of his head and pull sharply downward. Down he goes with a big crash, after which you slap on the cuffs. It's not a pretty technique, but who cares? It's one that takes advantage of the suspect's unbalance by adding energy to its direction.

From the Front

Approaching from the front is a little harder than from the

other directions because the suspect can more easily see you coming. Therefore, you have to be clever and catch him off guard. One method that works often, though not always, is to charge directly toward him. You want to startle him, so that he backpedals away from you and hopefully entangles his feet and loses his balance.

When this works perfectly, the suspect trips and falls after about three steps. When it doesn't work, it's usually because he has sidestepped your rush, or he is so coordinated that he can move back quickly without losing his balance. When he falls on his own, it's because the momentum of his kuzushi forced him down. If he trips but doesn't fall, you should nudge him in the direction of his kuzushi, forcing him the rest of the way down.

Another way to approach from the front is to do a foot sweep. If you are an experienced martial artist, you probably know how to execute one; if you are not, you will need to learn how from someone who does, since it's a technique that requires speed and dexterity.

I do sweep techniques by first nudging the suspect's shoulder or upper arm and follow an instant later by sweeping my front foot or rear foot against the side of his front foot. By nudging with my hand first, I force his attention high so I can sneak my low sweep in. Usually the sweep alone doesn't take the suspect down, but it does disrupt his balance and his thought process long enough for me to push his shoulder or upper arm in the direction of his kuzushi.

Here is another frontal approach that I especially like because it affects a suspect physically and psychologically. The technique calls for you to slap your suspect in the forehead, so obviously you need to be justified to use that level of force. You simply lunge toward the suspect and whack his forehead high around his hairline with your palm. You don't have to do it hard, since even a medium slap will snap his head back, and along with his head goes everything in his vision. Try this experiment. Look straight ahead; then with your eyes open, quickly look straight up to the ceiling and slightly behind you. Did you notice a slight, or not so slight, sense that your entire being was going to go

The officer deliberately backs up a volatile suspect until he trips over the stairs.
Then the officer quickly moves in to take advantage of the suspect's loss of balance.

over backwards? When you slap a suspect's forehead, it will feel to him as if he is going to do a backward somersault.

When you whack a suspect in the forehead, take advantage of his kuzushi and apply a takedown technique, such as a push on his upper chest, a tug on his shoulder, a trip, or any other technique you like. It won't take much.

Using Your Environment

Let's say you have been talking to a guy on the sidewalk and have decided to arrest him. Your sixth sense tells you that when you move in on him, he is going to make a run for it. However, since you just had a chili burger, you are in no condition to go jogging.

As you B.S. with him, subtly maneuver yourself into a position so that when you move toward him, he will step back and fall off the curb or bang into a mailbox or trip over a fire hydrant.

The idea is to use whatever environmental device that is available to throw him off balance so that he leans in one of the eight directions. When he does, move in quick as a wink and pull, push, tug, throw, do whatever, to force him further off balance and into your control.

If you are handling a domestic dispute and one of the parties has to go to jail, use a chair, stool, lamp, or the family pet to get the suspect unbalanced. If you are in a bar, be aware of all the tables, barstools, video poker machines, spittoons, and whatever else is available to you. Wherever you are, be aware of how your environment can help you do your job.

Mental Kuzushi

A friend of mine was a karate tournament champ in the 1960s, 1970s, and 1980s, fighting some of the biggest names around the United States and Japan. Besides his physical skills, he was adept at messing with his opponents' minds with such antics as patting them on top of the heads when they shook hands before their fight, laughing at them in a loud and abrasive cackle, and scoring on them with simplistic techniques that made them look foolish.

One time he was fighting another black belt champion for the grand championship title, a title that denotes the best of all the black belts. They were in the center ring, and after a couple of minutes of fast and furious exchanges, the score was tied, two to two. As the crowd sat on the edge of their seats, the two competitors squared off again and stalked each other like jungle cats. Suddenly my friend stopped moving around, turned his attention toward the crowd, and pointed at someone in the rear of the auditorium. With a puzzled look, his perspiring opponent also stopped and looked where my friend was pointing. In the blink of an eye, my friend buried his foot into the man's stomach, winning a point and the grand championship.

Here are a few methods you can use to mentally unbalance a suspect:

- Pointing away from you, as my friend did

- Screaming
- Shining your flashlight in his eyes
- Deliberately knocking something over, such as a table lamp, stack of dishes, a motorcycle
- Saying something to an imaginary partner behind the suspect
- Warning a suspect about a passing car
- Handing a suspect's ID back and then dropping it to the floor just before he takes it

The idea of these tricks is to take advantage of the suspect when he reacts to them in some fashion, such as when he turns away to look at the distraction or reaches out to catch something you have dropped or knocked over. You should move in quickly to force the suspect in the direction of his kuzushi. Most of the time, he won't be thrown physically off balance to any great degree, but he will be distracted or thrown off guard. Keep in mind that the opportunity will only exist for a short moment, so you need to be alert and move in quickly.

Acute pain can also be unsettling to a person's mental state. I'm not talking about wristlocks and other control holds, but acute pain applied to upset a person mentally. Say you are at a family fight call and the drunken husband is shouting his opinion of you in your face. He punctuates his comments with little pokes with his index finger against your chest. Since that's good enough for an arrest, you grab his pointer and give it a sharp twist, a maneuver that causes excruciating pain. He lets out a yelp and buckles his body in the direction of the pain. There is your opportunity. Seize the moment and push, nudge, or trip him in the direction of his kuzushi.

Here are other acute pain techniques that work well:

- Rap your knuckles on the small, vulnerable bones on the back of his hand.
- Step on his little toe with your boot heel.
- Flick your finger against the corner of his eye.
- Slap his Adam's apple.

- Pinch the skin on the inside of his upper arm or upper thigh.

These are all excruciatingly painful techniques that, while not debilitating, will shift a suspect's attention from you to himself. If the techniques cause physical kuzushi, actually disrupting the suspect's balance, all the better. If the techniques only cause mental kuzushi, that's OK, too, just as long as you take advantage of the opportunity.

Opportunities are like bubbles rising to the surface of a lake: they appear, pop, and then are gone forever.

Your Own Kuzushi

Always keep this thought in mind: you are subject to all the perils of kuzushi, too. Though you wear superhero's clothing and are highly trained in all the most recent crime fighting techniques, all that is useless if you are off balance and within easy reach of an attacker.

Will the average street dirtbag have heard of the Japanese word *kuzushi* or even understand its concept? Probably not. Nonetheless, if you are standing too close to him with your guard down and he attacks you, he may, just out of chance, catch you off balance.

Once a guy walked up to me while I was seated in my police car behind the wheel. I forget what we talked about, but I remember the conversation quickly went downhill and I decided to take him into custody. Without telling him to stand back, as I should have, I pushed open my door and swung my left leg out so I could stand up. Without warning, he pushed the car door into me, striking me in the upper body. While I was lucky and didn't get hurt from the impact, it nonetheless caught me in an extreme position of kuzushi, and I crashed into the door frame. It doesn't matter that the guy had no idea of kuzushi; he simply attacked me, and my kuzushi took over from there. In the five seconds that it took me to gasp from the sensation of having a steel door facing gouge my spine and then untangle myself from being half in and half out of the car, the suspect was long gone around the corner.

Be cognizant of how you stand when you talk to people, such as in the following situations:

- The foot-on-the-bumper position might be a classic police pose for writing a ticket, but it's a weak position that could get you dumped on your ass-phalt. You won't get knocked over if you keep both feet on the ground, angle your body to the suspect, and position yourself so the fender of the car is between you and the suspect.
- When you face a suspect straight on, rather than angling your body, you can easily be knocked over if he gives you a quick shove in the direction of your invisible support leg. An angled stance, which is similar to a boxer's stance, provides you with more stability against a shove.
- Even a slight nudge can send you tripping and sprawling if you stand with the back of your heels against a six-inch high curb. Instead, stand on the sidewalk while your opponent stands on the street. This prevents you from tripping over the curb, and it makes you taller, which gives you some psychological advantage.
- If you drop your pen, tell the suspect to step back before you pick it up. Not only are you off balance when you bend over, you may be placing your weapon within his easy reach.
- When making an arrest in a house, be aware of where you are in relation to coffee tables, planters, chairs, etc. If you are standing in front of a piece of furniture, a slight nudge against your chest can trip you or send you sprawling.

There are dozens of situations like these that you can find yourself in every day. While it's unrealistic to say that you will never be off balance, you need to always be aware of how you are standing and how you are moving when you are in close proximity to a potentially dangerous person. Be aware of your balance and where you are standing or walking at all times. Yes, it's one more thing for you to think about, but in time it will become a natural thought process that will keep you strong and stable.

HAVE A PLAN B

In my school, we call the act of moving from one grappling technique to another *flowing*. Police officers often call this their Plan B. But by whatever term it's called, it's absolutely paramount that you have a backup technique to go to if your first technique fails you. Oh, yours won't fail, you say? Yours is the absolute-bestest-technique ever invented, you say?

Bullshit, I say.

There is no technique that is absolute. Whenever I say this in class, there is always someone who says, "Oh yeah? What about a .45 slug to the head?" The heck-

Because this officer is facing the woman straight on, he can easily be knocked off balance.

ler then looks around at the other students and waits for a laugh and confirmation. I then tell them how many cases I've investigated where people have been shot in the head and continued to fight, including the guy who straddled his girlfriend by a service station gas pump and shot her multiple times in the face. She survived, recovered, and broke up with him. Another time, I had a call where a woman shot herself five times in the head but failed to kill herself and then fought like a tigress as we put her into an ambulance.

I've been practicing martial arts for more than three decades, and I've seen and experienced techniques that were excruciatingly painful, some of which hurt me for days afterward. But there have been times when I have used them on the street, only to have the suspect look at me as if I were just annoying him. One time, I thrust my index finger into the hollow of a guy's throat and leaned my body weight into it. He didn't scream and gasp for air as I thought he would, nor did his legs buckle as I had hoped. Instead, he just looked at me with a bored expression and said, "Ain't workin', is it?" Another time during a violent political demonstration, I hit a guy in the ribs with my side-handled baton with all the strength, speed, and proper body mechanics I could muster. Not only did he not react, he ignored me, didn't even look my way. That hurt my feelings.

Those techniques that hurt so much in a sterile training environment are not always felt on the street where alcohol, drugs, adrenaline, and insanity are powerful influences on a suspect's tolerance to pain. This is because the mind must receive messages from the body that it's being hurt. If the brain doesn't get the information, it isn't going to respond no matter what super-duper technique you do. So what is the answer? You flow into another technique. If the first one doesn't work, the second one might, and if that one doesn't do the job, you flow into a third. If that one fails, then you better run like the wind.

Any transition should be done smoothly and naturally. When you transition from one technique to another or even from one phase of a technique to the next, there is always an inherent risk because there is usually a brief loss of pain during the switch. Your objective is to transition in such a way so as to not draw attention to the loss of pain. Or if the suspect does realize it, he does so after you have already transitioned to the next technique.

In my agency, we teach about seven control holds. Although it's possible to transition from one to the other, time constraints prevent us from teaching how to do it. However, those officers who attend my martial arts school are taught how to transition from technique to technique because I want them to have a plan B and a plan C. Additionally, by learning how to flow smoothly, they increase their knowledge and understanding of the individual techniques.

With practice you can flow indefinitely from one technique to another with smoothness and only brief moments of reduced pain control. Here is an example of two transitions using three techniques. Beginning with the classic *sankayjo* wrist twist, you can easily flow into a technique called the judo lock. From here you can spin around and take the suspect to the ground, or you can slip your other arm behind his bent arm and apply a wrist-lock for handcuffing. The transitions are all smooth, there is little if any loss of control, and they conclude with the suspect positioned to be handcuffed.

FREE TIP: Here is a little secret that few people know. If you can flow smoothly from technique A to technique B, then you can flow from technique B to technique A. In other words, by simply reversing your flow, you now have another way to transition. When you begin examining techniques in your repertoire to see how they transition, see if you can also flow from your second technique back to the first. Most of the time you can. Cool, huh?

Changing the Angle

Say you apply a wrist flex technique, one that painfully stretches the wrist muscles and tendons beyond their range, a move that kills your partner's wrist in training, but surprisingly has no effect on your suspect. One solution is to quickly transition to another wrist technique that doesn't stretch the tendons but instead twists them. Some people can tolerate a stretch, but not a twist, and vice versa.

When Pain Doesn't Work

What if the suspect's mental state—drunk, high, deranged, enraged—affects his pain tolerance so that he doesn't feel anything, no matter what you do? When that happens, and it's all too common, you must switch to a leverage technique, one that doesn't rely on pain but the disruption of balance.

In my karate training, I like leg sweeps and eye gouging, assuming that if a guy can't see and can't stand up, he ain't gonna be too effective in a fight. Although in police work, you can't routinely gouge the eyes of an unruly suspect (although I know an officer who did in a survival situation, and it worked like a charm), you can sweep his feet and dump him onto his

When this wrist flex doesn't hurt the suspect, the officer jerks the suspect's arm straight and applies pressure against the elbow to leverage the man over.

back. You can dump him kindly, or you can dump him with extreme prejudice.

Let's say you applied a wristlock on a subject, but he doesn't feel it and jerks his arm out of the hold. Instead of attempting another pain compliance hold, you decide to take him to the ground to reduce resistance. You grab the back of his shoulder and pull down as you simultaneously sweep his closest foot, dumping his butt onto the concrete. This technique relies on balance or, more accurately, his loss of it.

Now that you've got him down, what are you going to do with him? First, try another pain technique. This time it might work because you are in a stronger position to apply greater pressure on his wrist. The instant he hits the floor, jerk him onto his side to reduce his options about what he can do to you with his arms and legs. Put one of your knees against his head, the other into his ribs, fold his arm, and apply a wrist flex. This is excruciatingly painful to most people because it's as if you are standing on a door and trying to open it. All of your pulling energy goes directly to those tender muscles and tendons on the back of your suspect's hand.

But if he tolerates this pain technique, you need to switch gears and go to a leverage movement. Quickly jerk his arm

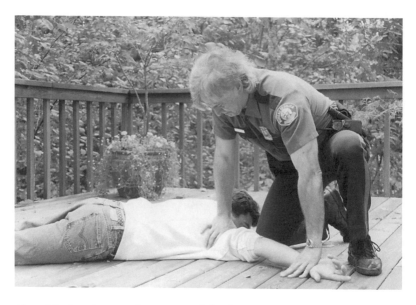

By positioning the suspect's arm toward the direction of his head about 45 degrees instead of straight out to the side and then pressing into his shoulder socket and on his wrist, it is virtually impossible for the suspect to get up.

straight up by his wrist and apply pressure one inch above his elbow joint. This isn't terribly painful, but it works as a leverage point that is hard for most to resist against. Hold on to his wrist tightly, push against the leverage point, and drive his arm into the floor, which will flop him over onto his stomach. Once he is prone and his arm is flat against the ground, move his arm forward, toward the direction of his head, so it forms a 45-degree angle to his body. This position acts as sort of a rudder and prevents most people from rolling over.

Hold his arm down with one hand on his wrist and your other on his elbow. While this is a powerful leverage position, you may opt to hold his head down instead of pushing against his elbow. Pushing his head into the floor has some leverage advantage, though you may have to push quite hard with some people. I asked one of my martial arts students, a 225-pound bodybuilder, to resist my push as I held his arm down in the 45-degree position with one hand and pushed against his head with

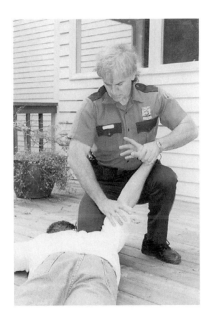

By applying pressure down on the suspect's wrist, hyperextending his elbow joint, and stretching his arm in his shoulder socket, you have just executed one of the strongest and most painful techniques in your repertoire.

my other. I was successful, but it took all of my strength. If he had been impervious to pain, it may not have worked.

A variation I have used on the street is to hold the suspect's arm flat on the floor with one of my hands, push down on his head with my other, and lean my shin bone against his triceps muscle, a couple of inches above his elbow joint. This is a strong position, and the shinbone on the triceps hurts intensely. If the suspect is a real asshole, you can move your shinbone back and forth as if sawing into his arm. This really hurts and makes many suspects squeal.

Another leverage point that works on most people who are lying in the prone position is at the top of the shoulder where the front, side, and rear shoulder muscles meet. As you hold the subject's arm down on the floor in the 45-degree position, blade your other hand and press where it forms a sort of pocket, or indentation. I could easily hold down my bodybuilder student by simultaneously pressing on this point and the ulna nerve just above the elbow joint.

Will these and other leverage points work on everyone? No. Will they work on most people? Yes. Try them—you'll like them.

MAKING TRANSITIONS WHEN HANDCUFFING

You can also do transitioning moves when you apply a technique that requires two or three steps. A good example is hand-cuffing techniques, since you first have to apply a control hold before you apply the cuffs.

Let's look at moving a prone subject's straight, upraised arm to the small of his back. There are several pain factors available to you as you hold his arm in the raised position, such as flexing his wrist, hyperextending his elbow, and moving his arm toward his head, which painfully strains the shoulder joint. But to handcuff him, you must move his arm to the small of his back where you can apply at least two more painful control holds. However, as you move his arm from the extended position to the bent position behind his back, there will be a brief moment where there is no pain. The trick then is to move his arm so that he is unaware of this glaring weakness in the technique. There are several ways to accomplish this.

Talk to the Suspect

Talk to your prisoner as you go through the handcuffing procedure, especially when you are transitioning from one position to another. When the suspect is listening to you, his mind is occupied with your words and their meaning, and since the human mind can only think of one thing at a time, your suspect has to make a mental switch to react to your brief transition period. By the time he realizes what you are doing and recognizes the transition as a weakness, you have successfully completed the movement. Ha, ha to him.

You can read him his Miranda rights, tell him what law he violated, tell him how he is the scum of the earth, or say anything else that keeps his mind occupied. Try asking him questions. For him to answer, he has to formulate his thoughts and then articulate them. Just don't allow any dead time between your question and his answer. He may not be thinking about what you asked, but rather how he is going to escape from your hold. Keep the questions coming so that he doesn't have time to think about resisting your handcuffing.

Speed Handcuffing

I have never been a fan of speed handcuffing because most

often it promotes sloppy form, which increases the risk of your screwing up the procedure and losing control of the prisoner. I have arrested countless people during my 29 years of law enforcement, and I can't recall once when handcuffing with great speed was a critical issue. On one occasion I was making an arrest while simultaneously getting bombarded with sticks and flying rocks from several dozen of the suspect's buddies. I used a pain compliance hold to control the suspect and to get him to come with me, and when we were away from his pals, I slapped on the handcuffs.

The ability to apply handcuffs smoothly is more important than applying them with great speed. The more you practice, the smoother you get, which results in some degree of quickness, anyway. Once you have the suspect in position to be handcuffed, you should be able to get the cuffs on in less than 15 seconds. That is fast enough, but not so much that you risk screwing up the process.

Smoothness plays an important part in transitioning. The smoother you are at it, which translates to some degree of quickness, the less chance the prisoner is going to recognize a weakness in your handcuffing.

Distraction

Distracting is simply forcing the prisoner to think of one thing while you do something else. If you have hold of the prisoner's right arm as he lies in the prone, order him to look to his left. As he turns his head, take advantage of this brief distraction and move his right hand to the small of his back for handcuffing. It's a brief distraction, so you want to immediately take advantage of it and put your transition into motion.

Here is a little distraction trick I used to do when I worked skid row. You can still use it today if you are careful about whom you use it against and who is watching you. Be warned that you definitely run the risk of getting a complaint or being sued because it looks worse than it is. You didn't learn it from me. Here is how it works.

When I had a suspect prone on the sidewalk, and I was struggling to get his arms behind his back because he was tensing up or holding them under his body, I would flick the corner of his eye with my finger. I never poked him in the eye, though I would come very near it: to the side, above, or under it. It was a simple technique that took advantage of the fact that most people are squeamish about their eyes. My flick would make the suspect flinch and jerk his head away. Then when he was thinking about his vision and not stiffening his muscles, I jerked his arm to wherever I wanted it.

I mention this eye-flicking concept only as an example of distraction, not to suggest a technique.

Here is another example. In my agency, we teach a standing handcuffing method that begins with the suspect's fingers interlaced behind his head. You take hold of, say, his right hand and swing it down to the small of his back, while his left hand remains on top of his head. There are two things you need to be concerned about with this method: there is virtually no pain as his hand is carried from his head to his back, a point in the process where the suspect could resist if he realized the weakness, and it's an almost automatic response for the prisoner to want to lower his left hand when you move his right one. This is a no-no since you don't have control over it.

Here is how we prevent this, killing two birds with one stone, so to speak. As you reach up and cover the back of his right hand with your right palm, grasp any one finger on his left hand, which is interlaced with his right, and tell him to keep his left hand on top of his head. Simultaneously, bend the finger back just enough to give him a shot of discomfort. This briefly distracts his mind from what is happening to his right hand. By the time he realizes what is going on, you have him in a strong wristlock and in a good position to apply a powerful pain compliance hold.

Sometimes you have to turn up the pain a little to help make a transition. Say you are standing next to the suspect, one hand holding his upper arm, the other holding his wrist. As you begin to push his arm back to the center of his back for handcuffing, he balks at the idea by stiffening his arm. Instantly, you drive your knee into his peroneal nerve, which is found halfway down the side of the thigh, about where the stripe on a uniform trouser is. This is a highly vulnerable nerve that hates to be struck. Hit it hard and your man will be down on his knees; hit it with medium force and the pain will distract him sufficiently to give you a moment to get his arm behind his back.

We have been talking about a variety of techniques, principles, and concepts. Now let's look at one of the best training devices for practicing and teaching them that makes learning fun and, most importantly, beneficial.

MONKEY LINE

I don't recall where I first learned the concept of monkey line, probably from one of the Chinese fighting arts I've studied, or maybe from arnis, the Filipino martial art that uses it extensively. Wherever I got it, I'm most grateful because I've used it in my martial arts and police defensive tactics classes for years, relying heavily on its versatility for training and the benefits my students get from it. Monkey line can be used to work hand techniques, kicks, grappling, blocks, police baton, and defense against guns, knives, and sticks. It can be used whether there are six people in the class or a dozen.

One of its many attributes is that it allows you to practice a technique on a variety of people. For example, one 10-rep set can be practiced on 10 partners of varying physique types: short, tall, heavy, slight, male, female, long-armed, short-armed, flexible, and stiff. This is beneficial because the greater the number of partners you can train with, the greater your understanding of a given technique.

How It's Done

Let's say you want to practice a technique against a suspect who is reaching toward your badge. No doubt you have had people threaten to tear your badge from your shirt and pin it somewhere else where it would really hurt. While most of the time this is just an idle threat, the next person who says it just may be capable of carrying it out.

Consider a simple defense against a badge grab: the suspect reaches toward your chest, you swat his hand aside and follow up with a control hold of your choice.

As with any new technique, you would first practice it one-on-one with the same partner until you get the hang of it. Once you can apply it effortlessly, you are ready to practice with several people in the monkey line.

Stand and face a column of students who are also facing you. One at a time, each student will step up to you and thrust his arm forward toward your chest as if to tear off your badge. Smack the hand aside, do whatever footwork is necessary to get in position, and apply the wristlock. Once that person yelps, slaps out, or somehow indicates that you have applied sufficient pressure, you should release the hold. He then moves to the rear of the line, and you get ready for the next person to move up and reach for your badge.

By the time you have worked your way through the column, you will have practiced the technique on, say, 10 different training partners, all of whom react differently to your moves. For example, you swat one student's reaching arm, and it flies across its owner's chest, but when you swat the next one's hand, it moves only an inch or two. Or when you bend one student's arm at the elbow, it folds easily, but with the next student you have to use considerably more force. You will also discover differences in the flexibility of each student's wrist and differences in each student's pain threshold.

If you always train with the same partner, you will never experience these important differences, and if you only change partners once or twice during a class, it would take several classes to give you this broader experience. But in the time it takes you to go through the monkey line just once—about three minutes—you experience training with 10 people of various sizes and shapes. Take another trip through the monkey line and you will have practiced 20 repetitions with 10 partners in six to eight minutes. That is an excellent use of training time.

You are limited only by your imagination about how you can use the monkey line. Here are two more ways I use frequently.

Attack Recognition

Untrained officers (and many who are trained) don't see the suspect's fist until after it's rushing toward their faces. Of course, that is better than not seeing the fist at all, since you just might have a chance to duck or block it. But that's quite chancy, especially if you are having an off day or the suspect is having an especially good day. Ideally, you want to see that fist long before it makes your face look like a dropped, overripe cantaloupe.

Is there a way to train to see an attack earlier so that you have an increased response time? Yes, there is. After all, the fist had to begin someplace; it had to start from what I call the position of origin. Let me explain with an example.

A man is clearly upset that you stopped him on the street: his hands are on his hips, and he's copping a major attitude. Without warning, his fist suddenly launches straight toward your formerly extraordinarily good-looking face.

Here is another example. You are in a tavern checking the ID of a guy sitting with his arm resting on the bar. Without warning, a huge fist at the end of that same arm rushes code three toward your proud jaw.

In both scenarios, the punch was launched without warning, right? Wrong. The warning was there; you just didn't recognize it.

Most people telegraph their punch by first moving their shoulders, head, chest, or entire upper body. They might telegraph by twitching their mouth, dipping their shoulder, lifting their shoulder, inhaling or exhaling sharply, rotating their chest, or leaning their upper body forward. Even highly trained fighters do these things, though they train to do them with subtlety or do them so quickly that the movements are virtually imperceptible. Untrained people, like the hotheaded motorist above, or the bar patron whose courage has been fortified with beer, usually telegraph with all the subtlely of beating on a base drum. Since there are a huge variety of skill levels among fighters on the street, the monkey line is an especially valuable tool to help you experience all the variations in telegraphing.

Partial Movement

Stand in front of a column of fellow students in your standard interview position as if you were dealing with a routine, low-level threat on the street. The first student steps in front of you, close enough to strike you in the face. As you watch him, he moves his arm as if to punch, but he only extends it a few inches, about one-quarter or less of the distance toward your face. Your job is to watch for everything that moves: his shoulder, head, mouth, chest, and opposite arm. You don't do anything other than watch because the exercise is only to educate your eyes about what all moves at the origin of a punch.

Stories about old China and Japan tell of masters who had a sixth sense and could tell what an attacker was going to do before he moved. Nonsense. What these masters had developed was an educated eye as to the subtleties that occur before an attack is launched. You too can learn to recognize a punch or kick in its earliest stage by practicing this exercise.

The monkey line is a great training device because you get to experience the same partial attack from a variety of people. While it's true that some students have their own individual ways of moving, nonetheless they will all exhibit certain similarities. It won't take long for your training to pay off, usually only two or three sessions. You will quickly begin to recognize the movements, subtle and not so subtle, that precede an attack and be able to react to them with a jam, an avoidance move, a block, or whatever.

Redman Training

There are different versions of training with body padding around the country, though all share certain basics. One training officer puts on a suit that pads him from head to toe and then commences to get the crap beat out of him by officers armed with police batons. In my department it's called "redman training" because the suit consists of heavy red padding similar to the protective equipment karate people wear on their hands and feet.

Several years ago, I participated in a class for defensive tactics instructors in which people from the ASP baton company taught us not only how to use the telescopic baton but how to teach it too. The class consisted of a lengthy warm-up, basic nomenclature, footwork, techniques to carry and draw the weapon, ways to strike, and ways to move and parry. During the final hour, an instructor donned the redman suit and stood in the center of the training area. One by one, the student instructors were pitted against the redman who would continually advance no matter how many times he was struck with the ASP. The redman and each student clashed for a minute the first round and 45 seconds the second round. At the conclusion of the rounds the students were drenched with sweat, breathing like workhorses, and were totally exhausted.

At the end of the workshop, everyone was ecstatic over how tired and sweaty they were. There were lots of comments about the great training, and how they felt so wonderfully exhausted. Well, I was tired too, but I saw the training differently. I thought it sucked. At least the last hour.

As I've taught over the years, I've noticed that students all too often translate their fatigue at the end of a class to mean they had good training. I disagree. Intense fatigue doesn't necessarily mean that the training was good. It can, but not always. Bad training can be fatiguing, too.

Until this ASP training, we had been using the side-handled baton, a weapon we were unsatisfied with. Part of the ASP training was designed to sell the bureau instructors on the telescopic baton, and, because too many people equate fatigue with good training, that was the approach they took. Didn't fool me, though. I'm too sharp for that—and humble too.

I thought the training left everyone with sloppy technique and with a conscious or subconscious belief that their blows didn't work. This is because after we spent several hours perfecting our stances and strikes in the air and on pads, we were pitted against the redman, who never reacted to our hits, but instead aggressively advanced on us no matter what we did. This caused a sort of desperation with some students, followed by the disintegration of their carefully practiced techniques. Since we had just learned the movements in the past three hours, there was not enough time to ingrain them into our reflexes. As the seconds ticked by and our lungs burned from fatigue, many students' precision movements went down the toilet and they ended up whacking madly at this red thing that wouldn't die. This wouldn't have happened if the redman portion of the training had included the monkey line. Here is how the training could have been done better.

The redman stands in front of the monkey line. As each ASP-carrying officer steps forward, he responds to a different stimulus thrown by the redman, such as a typical street drunk's wild swinging punch. The officer responds with a block or an evasive movement and then counters with an ASP strike to the legs or a strike to the attacking arm and then a follow-up strike to the legs. The type of response should initially be determined by the instructor, using strikes and thrusts that have previously been practiced in the air and against striking shields.

After everyone goes through the monkey line two or three times, the redman's attack changes to, say, a kick. This time the officer responds by shuffling out of the way and countering with a strike to the attacking leg or whatever other response ordered by the instructor.

The number and variety of attacks by the redman and how the officers respond to them are determined by the instructor or the students. The redman can punch, kick, push, charge, run away, or do a cartwheel. The officers respond using those techniques learned in the drills practiced earlier in the class.

The last exercise against the redman is unstructured, though it does have a couple of limitations. It's unstructured in that the redman is free to attack each student in the monkey line any way he chooses. For example, he might punch at the first student and then try to tackle the next one. The drill is limited because the redman will attack only with one or two techniques. Though the students have to respond under pressure to an unknown attack, it's not as relentless as in the training I received and described earlier.

This somewhat controlled unstructuredness prevents students from getting frustrated and forgetting all of their new techniques. With this approach, students leave the training session with confidence that what they learned will help them on the street, as opposed to my initial redman training, which was not conducive to positive learning.

The monkey line is an excellent training device that condenses training time and allows students to practice against a variety of people. Let your imagination run wild and you will be pleased to see how many ways the monkey line can be used.

Chapter 5

Do Whatever It Takes to Survive

CALIFORNIA HIGHWAY PATROL SURVIVAL CREED

The will to live, to survive the attack
Must be uppermost in every officer's mind.

Fight back against all odds.
Turn the tables on your attacker.
Don't quit. Get up off the ground.
Seize the initiative. Take every advantage.
Kick. Punch. Scratch. Bite.
Don't give up!

You're going to hurt. You're going to bleed.
But don't quit. Don't give up!
You're going to make it.

You're not just fighting for God and Country;
You're fighting for yourself,

For your family,
For your life.
If the attacker knocks your teeth out,
Swallow them and keep fighting.

Don't let them kill you on some dirty freeway.

Anonymous author, probably a California Highway Patrol officer

WHEN THE CACA HITS THE FAN

What if you suddenly found yourself in a situation where you had to fight for your life? Not with firearms, not with SWAT's help, not with a half-dozen backup units screaming code three to your aid. I'm talking about a life-and-death struggle between you and an asshole who could care less about your shiny badge and crisply ironed uniform.

The kind of fight I'm talking about here doesn't happen often. Although you may get into a hundred, perhaps a thousand fights during your law enforcement career, few, if any, of them will be a desperate struggle for your life. Most of the time you fight to prevent a suspect from escaping or to elicit cooperation from a suspect (I love that term: *elicit cooperation*).

Although there are no statistics, I would guess that most officers go through their careers without being involved in a life-and-death struggle, a fight where the officer knows that if he doesn't win, he will definitely be seriously injured or killed.

I know an officer who freely admits that he screwed up his approach to a suspect, which resulted in a desperate struggle for his service revolver. It began when the officer approached the man to take him into custody. But in the blink of an eye, the suspect grabbed the butt of the officer's gun and began pulling it out of his holster. Fortunately, the officer was quick enough to get his hands over the suspect's hands, a move he had practiced often in his defensive tactics classes. The man was still able to get the weapon partially out, but the officer's practiced technique prevented him from removing it further.

They struggled fiercely for several minutes, the suspect's hands on the butt of the gun, the officer's hands locked in a death grip over the suspect's. At one point, the man managed to get one hand free and repeatedly punched the officer's face and head area. The struggling pair fell to the ground where the officer continued to hold on to the butt of his gun with all his strength.

Just as the officer's strength began to wane, he took advantage of a split-second window of opportunity. He quickly withdrew his portable belt radio with one hand, while continuing to lock the suspect's hand with the other, and slammed the steel-cased radio into the suspect's head, once, twice, several times. That was enough to get him to release his grip and give the officer an opportunity to draw his weapon and hold the man at gunpoint until reinforcements arrived.

Citizens Won't Always Help

Never count on citizens to help you. In fact, it's a good idea not to expect their help at all. If they do come to your aid, consider it an anomaly, a cherry on the pudding that rarely happens.

I once got into a fight with a Hell's Angel motorcycle outlaw that went on for several minutes. It began just after I stopped him for a traffic violation and discovered that he had a warrant out of California. As I started to call for backup, he decided to leave, which I couldn't allow.

As we battled like pit bulls, there were a few moments when I thought I was going to lose. He continually shot hungry looks at my gun as we crashed into the side of the police car and then rolled up on the hood and down on the pavement. Though there was no doubt in my police-trained mind that he wanted my gun, I was not about to let him have it. When the moment presented itself, I went for a carotid restraint and sent him into la-la land.

I handcuffed him, dragged the big oaf over to my car, and stuffed him into the backseat. I slammed the door shut and, with a deep breath of exhaustion, collapsed against the side of the fender. It was then that I noticed all the people. I had made the traffic stop in a bank parking lot near a busy intersection. Now every lane in the street was jammed with stopped cars, their occupants watching with their mouths hanging open at my fierce struggle. There were several people on the sidewalk, too, standing dumbly and watching me as if I were a sidewalk juggler. I was pissed.

To cap it off, a motorist laughed loudly out his window and shouted, "Hey officer, want some help?"

Out of total reflex and a loss of all sense of professionalism, I shouted back, "Go have sex with yourself!" or words similar to those.

Getting into any physical confrontation is an adrenaline rush, whether you are bending a guy's wrist joint or dragging him out of his car by his throat. But it's a whole different ball game when you are convinced that if you don't win the fight, you just might end up taking a cold dirt nap forever.

You probably have thought about what you would do if a drunk stiffened his arm when you grabbed it or how you would react if the female half of a domestic fight tried to whack her old man with a frying pan in your presence. But have you thought about what you would do in a life-and-death struggle, armed only with your bare hands? Do you know all your physical capabilities? Do you recognize all your weaknesses?

Far too many officers bury their heads in the sand and either ignore the possibility that they could get into a life-and-death struggle or convince themselves that they will always prevail because their natural instincts will take over and carry them to victory. Denial may be a comfortable way to think, but it can get you seriously killed. You must accept the possibility that someday, possibly today or maybe not for another 10 years, you might have to fight for your life.

You have probably read the statistics: tens of thousands of officers are injured every year in this country because of physical confrontations. Some are crippled, some are killed. It happens in the concrete jungles of the big cities, and it happens in the dusty roads of farm communities. It happens to officers who are not as good as you are at your job, and it happens to officers who are better. Accept the possibility that it can happen anytime and anywhere.

Never, ever get into the mind-set that you will instinctually fight well, especially if you have never trained for an all-out fight for survival, or if you have never even thought about it.

Are You Capable of Taking a Life with Your Bare Hands?

It is important that you think about whether you can take another person's life with your bare hands. Shooting a suspect to death from 20 feet away, or even at three feet, can be a traumatic experience, one that can affect you and your family for a lifetime (read *Deadly Force Encounters*).

Taking the life of another with your bare hands can be equally as traumatic, possibly more so. You should be clear in your mind that you are capable of choking, beating, or stomping a suspect to death if it means saving your life or another's. For sure, it's not a pleasant thought, and it's something that rarely happens, but you need to be self-aware. You need to know the answer.

If after thinking about it long and hard the answer is no, then you need to seriously consider whether you should be doing police work.

Be Able to Eat Some Pain

It is always amazing to me when a new karate student acts startled the first time his training partner whacks him in the chest or shoulder with a padded glove. Sometimes the person will look at me with total surprise and amazement as if to say, "What is going on here? Am I going to get hit in karate?"

Hello! You are in a class learning how to fight. We are not playing checkers, and we are not learning how to arrange pretty flowers. WE ARE TRAINING TO FIGHT. You are probably going to get whacked from time to time by your fellow students, but if by some fluke you don't, I will make sure that you get that experience. If I didn't give it to you, I would be ripping you off as your teacher. If you don't get hit in class, what do you think is going to happen out on the street the first time you get smacked when fighting a resisting suspect? What honest martial artists have reported is that they froze, shocked by the fact that they were hit. They had trained in a school where contact was not allowed. They freaked the first time they felt even a mild blow, and their assailants quickly took advantage of the moment. It is important that you get desensitized to getting hit. Some police academies expose the recruits to boxing while wearing large gloves to allow the students to feel what it is like to get hit. This is a good idea. Desensitization can also be achieved by having a training partner hit you with hand pads, padded sticks, open-hand slaps, or any other object that doesn't cause injury, but still lets you feel the sensation of impact. In my private school, we practice drills where one student lands a fairly hard punch or kick, and the student receiving the blow responds by immediately hitting back. The idea is to untrain the natural "ouch" response and replace it with a counterstrike.

You should mentally accept the fact that in a fight with a resisting suspect, you may get injured. It might be a strained muscle, a wrenched finger, a poked eye, a skinned knuckle, or a knot on your forehead from a big, hairy fist sandwich. Accept this as a reality, so that when it happens, you are mentally able to continue to function and get the job done.

The Japanese have a saying: "When you break your arm, hide it from your enemy in your sleeve." In other words, don't let the suspect see your injury. If it hurts, so be it. Eat the pain and continue to do your job.

Your life may depend on it.

IMPORTANT COMBAT ELEMENTS

Let's examine several elements of survival fighting that are important to think about, discuss with other officers, and incorporate into your training. You may have never considered some of them before and probably have never seen them in your agency's defensive tactics program. You should think about them, though, and they should be taught in your training. They are fighting concepts taken from the martial arts, and, as such, they work well when the name of the game is survival. They may not all be politically correct with some agency's fuzzy, huggy approach to police work. Nonetheless, they are important to your goal of returning to your home at the end of the shift.

What You Should Look For

One significant element of fighting that is often ignored in police defensive tactics training is where to look when you are face-to-face with a combative suspect. It's an important element because by knowing how to look correctly you can prevent embarrassment, the escape of your prisoner, and getting your nose shoved somewhere behind your ear.

American custom teaches us to look into the eyes of the person we are talking with, but in a fight this can prevent you from recognizing the suspect's telegraphic signals that indicate he is going to attack or flee. By not looking at his eyes, but instead looking at his upper chest and shoulders, you can actually see what he is going to do a split second before he does it. This is because every fighter, no matter how highly trained, gives signals (sometimes glaring ones, sometimes subtle) that indicate he is going to move in a certain fashion. Most of these signals are given by the upper torso.

The Suspect's Upper Body

By gazing at the suspect's shoulders and upper chest area, you can determine what he is going to do. These movements are subtle, but with experience, you can learn to read them and know what they mean. For example, let's assume the suspect is facing you in the classic boxer's stance, a position used by trained fighters and mimicked by untrained fighters in every other beer pub in the country.

Here are some points to watch for:

- If his chest rotates counterclockwise while his shoulders stay stationary, he is going to throw a right-hand punch to your upper body or head.
- If his chest rotates counterclockwise as his shoulders dip forward, look for a right-hand technique to your abdomen or groin.

- If his shoulder angles backward as his chest rotates counterclockwise, he is going to throw a right kick.
- If his chest rotates clockwise and his shoulders stay stationary, he will punch with his lead arm.
- If his chest rotates clockwise and his shoulders angle backward, he is getting ready to kick with his front leg.
- If he suddenly lifts his upper body, look for him to charge you.

The Suspect's Breathing

By watching the suspect's upper body, you can easily monitor his breathing. Look for this: he will usually launch his attack at the conclusion of his inhalation. It's difficult for a fighter to attack or even defend himself after he exhales. What this means is this: if you are going to go on the offensive, such as rushing forward to grab, punch, or kick the suspect, you will increase your chance of success by moving when he is at the bottom of his exhalation.

The Suspect's Eyes

Although the eyes do communicate information, you need to be careful not to look at them for too long. If your suspect is a good street fighter, he may know how to use his eyes to fake you. For example, a poor fighter will look at your groin before he kicks there, but a good fighter will look there to get you to react in some way to protect the area and then launch a punch at your face.

I find that it works best to look back and forth from the suspect's eyes to his shoulder/chest area. The face area of the average, nontrained fighter will usually show that he is going to attack, such as when he inhales sharply, squints his eyes, tenses his face muscles, tightens his lips, grits his teeth, or angles his head. I then flick my eyes back to his shoulder/chest area to read what that attack will be.

Sometimes I will step back out of his hitting range for a moment and look at his eyes to read his mental condition: fear, rage, confusion, and any signs of weakness. Is he darting

The German shepherd stare, where the suspect looks off to the side rather than at you, often precedes an attack.

his eyes around as if looking for an avenue of escape? Is he looking me up and down as if sizing me up to devour me like a ham sandwich?

The German Shepherd Stare

While in the army, I was a dog handler for a year in the Florida Everglades before Uncle Sam decided I was needed in Vietnam. I learned quickly that when dogs get pissed, they often look off to the side of you. This communicates in their unique little doggy language that in a moment or two, they are going to rip your ass to shreds. Besides the stare, I learned that some dogs emit a low-level growl that also telegraphs that flesh tearing was imminent.

I've seen suspects do this, too. Just like a German shepherd, they stare hard off to the side and become still. I've even had a couple of them growl, though usually they just grit their teeth. Every time I have seen a suspect do this, he has fought as fiercely as a German shepherd, too.

Watch for Darting Eyes

On the flip side of the German shepherd stare is the suspect who, as you talk to him, looks all around instead of directly at you. He might be looking for an escape route, or he might be looking for a weapon to use against you. If he is a knowledgeable fighter, be aware that he may try to distract you by getting you to look in the same direction he is looking, and then take advantage when you fall for it by sucker-punching you in the kisser.

A fellow officer had a suspect do that, and a second later the suspect pulled a Saturday night special, pointed it at the officer's chest, and squeezed the trigger four times. Luckily, the firing pin fell lightly on all four cartridges, and the gun didn't fire.

My friend's gun did, though.

What You Should Do

Monitor Your Eyes

Be aware of where you are looking so you don't give off signals as to your intentions. If the suspect appears anxious as you begin to talk about arresting him, avoid looking at his arm before you take hold of it. Instead, you may want to look at his other arm or shoot a quick glance off to his far side. This will distract him ever so slightly, moving his mind away from the place you are going to take hold of.

When you are in a fight for survival and delivering blows with your baton, hands, or feet, don't look where you intend to hit. If the suspect has any street savvy at all, he will instantly read your intentions and take measures to defend himself.

Move to the Suspect's Lead-Arm Side

Here is a little tip that you can consider when you are practicing ways to approach a suspect you want to put your hands on and handcuff. Say the suspect has assumed a left-side-forward position, one similar to the classic boxer's stance. Step toward his left side, using whatever technique you have been taught to close the distance. Stepping to the suspect's "outside" makes it relatively easy for you to get his lead arm, since it's the closest one to you and places you in a "safe zone" away from the front of his body where he can more easily kick and punch you.

Get Behind Him
As an add-on to the last concept, think about getting behind the suspect whenever possible. Even an untrained person can hit to his front with his legs and fists, but it takes training or random luck to successfully hit to the rear.

CAROTID RESTRAINT

There is a reason so many police agencies no longer allow carotid restraint techniques, neck holds that restrict blood flow to the suspect's brain: these holds tend to kill people.

There was an unfortunate death in my agency a few years ago when an officer used a carotid constraint to prevent a large, violent man from hurting another officer, whom he had just pushed away, and several citizens he had been harassing (the officer's account of this incident is detailed in *Deadly Force Encounters*). The restraint hold worked, and the big man went to sleep on the pavement. But a few minutes later he was dying, and a few minutes after that he was dead. Because the officer was white and the suspect was black, the city went crazy for a few weeks. Of course, the media fueled the incident into a full-blown circus, and all the local politicians jumped through hoops for angry voters who couldn't fathom that a police officer would strangle an ex-serviceman and a father of two children.

Although all the bleeding hearts screamed that the carotid restraint hold is a killing technique, the truth is that judo and jujitsu fighters render each other unconscious regularly using a variety of carotid- and windpipe-constriction holds. In fact, one fighting art boasts 75 different ways to render unconsciousness. Yet, while I have known karate fighters who have died of kicks to the body, I have never heard of death from a carotid constraint hold in the grappling arts since I began training in 1965.

But then martial artists are generally in better health than the average suspect who is acting out so violently that it's necessary to render him unconscious. Add to that the effects of drugs, especially cocaine, and you now have a person highly susceptible to problems from carotid constraint.

Here is a brief list of people at risk:

- Men over the age of 40
- Older people with cardiac abnormalities
- People with a history of seizures
- People who use alcohol and street drugs, especially PCP, LSD, mescaline, amphetamines, and cocaine
- People taking prescription drugs with side effects predisposing them to cardiac arrhythmia

Suspects who are violent and under the influence of cocaine or suspects in an extreme state of mental agitation are highly vulnerable to what the medical profession calls "sudden unexpected death." Add to this a carotid constraint hold, and you greatly increase the chance of the suspect's day coming to a screaming halt. But the catch-22 is that the person exhibiting this kind of behavior is the very person you should be rendering unconscious for your safety—and his safety, too.

Cocaine-Induced Excited Delirium

The worse kind of cocaine abuse for police officers is cocaine-induced excited delirium, which is also called cocaine psychosis. Although most people under the influence will respond to medical treatment, cocaine-induced excited delirium is usually regarded as a potentially lethal medical emergency. The drug stimulates both the central nervous and cardiovascular systems, and it constricts blood vessels, elevates the heart rate, and increases blood pressure. These effects have caused death even to people who didn't have preexisting health problems, and, not surprisingly, these effects can cause substantial problems for an already diseased heart or cardiovascular system.

Suspects experiencing cocaine-induced excited delirium typically exhibit intense paranoia, followed by violent, bizarre behavior. Often, the suspect will display violence against inanimate objects (particularly glass, for some odd reason), and they run amok, scream, and strip off their clothing. An additional symptom of concern to police officers is that they often exhibit great strength and appear not to feel pain.

One day a man in one of our courtrooms flipped out because of this condition. He ran out of the building, stripped off his clothing, and streaked down the sidewalk, breaking windows along the way. When the police got there, he made a bad decision and sprinted across the street and into the Justice Center, a building that houses 16 floors of police offices. Several officers took him down in a hallway and fought his tremendous strength with restraint holds before they could get him cuffed. Though he was never struck with a fist or a baton, and carotid constraint was not used, he died a few minutes later.

Excited Delirium

Excited delirium without the supplement of drugs is caused by the suspect's mental condition, usually sparked by extreme agitation. The acting-out symptoms are virtually the same as those of cocaine psychosis.

Here are a few signs that may be a result of cocaine-induced excited delirium or excited delirium caused by extreme mental agitation:

- Delirium
- Violent behavior
- Superhuman strength
- Dilated pupils
- Paranoia
- Hearing voices
- High body temperature
- Stripping clothes
- Seizures
- Hiding
- High pulse rate
- Aggression toward objects

- Breaking glass
- Profuse sweating
- Swearing

Suspects experiencing excited delirium are highly susceptible to dying from the use of the carotid constraint. In fact some experts believe that most suspects who died of what was attributed to carotid restraint most likely died of sudden unexpected death syndrome.

There are more inherent risks when applying the carotid constraint on the street than there are in the relatively sterile environment of a martial arts school. A suspect tends to fight much more intensely than martial arts students, which often puts more of a strain on his neck. Here are some risk factors besides those that exist with excited delirium:

- Brain damage can occur if blood flow is restricted for more than three minutes.
- Rough application can cause injury to the larynx or trachea.
- Jerking or tilting the head after the hold is applied can cause injury.
- Damage to the hyoid bone will cause swelling and blockage of the windpipe.
- If the vargus nerves, which are located in the same area as the carotid arteries, are stimulated or depressed, it may cause momentary, irregular heart activity. This could cause problems for people with heart ailments or young people under age 14 who have underdeveloped nervous systems.
- If the carotid constraint is done on a standing suspect, his unconscious weight will drop onto your arm, potentially injuring his neck.
- Don't apply this restraint to a victim more than twice in a 24-hour period.
- Mental disorientation and coughing usually occur for a few minutes.

I present this information here for your knowledge, not to

DO WHATEVER IT TAKES TO SURVIVE

cause you hesitation in the use of the carotid restraint. It's important that you give thought to using or not using the carotid restraint since there are lots of drug users on the street as well as hordes of mentally ill people. The possibility of your running into one or the other is 100 percent. When and if to use the carotid restraint is a decision that only you can make, considering all the elements of the situation. In my agency, officers can use it only in situations where deadly force would be justified. This is unfortunate because it's a valuable tool for officers in overcoming violent resistance when other methods are insufficient and when the only other option is the firearm.

I encourage you to seek out one or two methods of applying carotid restraint holds. Even if your agency has banned them, as mine has, they are still important techniques for survival. Knowing how to apply a carotid restraint is important and so is knowing what to do after your suspect is sleeping away at your feet.

I have put students out in four seconds, but those were ideal circumstances. Normally, it takes about 20 seconds once the hold is applied correctly, and most often they regain consciousness in about 15 to 30 seconds. Sometimes people are not even aware they went out and will wake up completing a sentence that got interrupted by the constraint hold.

Since you never know how long a suspect is going to be unconscious, you want to get him handcuffed immediately. Get him onto his back or side, then check for vital signs: pulse and breathing. If these things are faint or nonexistent, you need to do CPR and call for paramedics. Even if his signs are fine, but he has suffered some kind of trauma from the hold, or he informs you he has a medical condition that might have been aggravated by the technique, have him checked by medical personnel.

Do not lay the suspect down on his stomach in the car. Sit him up and keep him under constant observation as he is transported to jail. Be sure to notify jail personnel that a carotid restraint hold was used, and note it in your report. Explain exactly why you did it and how you did it. Don't forget or hide any details in your report that a defense attorney can use against you.

HITTING

Let's talk about something your administration and the citizens you serve don't want to talk about or, for that matter, even think about: hitting people. The brass and the taxpayers are not sure what they want you to do when you are up to your crack in alligators, since most of them have never had the displeasure of alligators nipping at them. Nonetheless, they are positive they don't want you to hit people.

Well, the hell with them. As the old axiom says: "I'd rather be tried by twelve than carried by six." If hitting the suspect means you will survive the fight, then go ahead and hit and deal with the whiners later. Always keep in the forefront of your mind that as you begin each work shift, your primary objective is to go home at the end of it. If you gotta smack a few folks during the day to accomplish this goal, so be it.

How to Hit with Your Hands

Here's a war story about hitting with your hands. My partner and I got into a car pursuit that ended when the suspect drove up the rear of a parked car in such a way that his vehicle was sent rocketing straight up about 15 feet into the air. As cool and spectacular as the crash was, the suspect was not only uninjured, he climbed out of the wreckage ready to fight. He grabbed my partner and did a Hercules technique on him, lifting him overhead about an arm's length and tossing him aside like an unwanted stepchild.

I was two steps behind my 6-foot-3-inch partner, and when I saw the suspect so casually toss him through the air, I knew right away that a wristlock wouldn't be enough to take this guy down. Just as I got to him, the suspect slipped on the wet grass and went down onto one knee. Seizing the moment, I drove my fist into the back of his head.

Bad move. The knuckle on my little finger shattered like a fine piece of China, though the blow barely slowed the guy down. After a lengthy struggle, we managed to get him controlled and handcuffed. I had to go to the hospital to get my hand put into a cast and then back to the precinct where my peers were merciless with their ribbing, all of which could have been avoided if I had hit the suspect correctly.

Karate fighters are taught to punch with their two large knuckles. Take a moment to make a fist and look at the back of your hand. Notice how your index and middle knuckles are supported by the mass of your hand, wrist, and forearm. Now look at your little knuckle and see how it's not supported at all, which explains why it breaks so easily and why you shouldn't hit with your clenched fist unless you are highly trained.

So, why did I break my hand? Didn't I know how to hit properly? Actually, I did. At the time that I hit the bozo, I was a second-degree black belt with about 14 years of training. While it's possible that I simply screwed up and wasn't holding my hand correctly, it's an absolute that the human head is a risky target to hit (so is a bull's head for that matter). John Wayne got away with punching guys in the face without hurting his hand, but then John Wayne got away with many things that mortal guys like us could and should never do.

In my book *Anything Goes*, I wrote extensively about how you should hit if you insist on using your fist. I talk about how it's better to hit a person in the body—such as the neck, upper chest, nipple area, solar plexus, ribs, and the kidneys—since these targets are so much softer than the head, which reduces the risk to your knuckles and wrist. But if you like to live on the edge and insist on punching to a guy's hard skull, there are photos in *Anything Goes* that show how flat the head is around the ears, making the ear a far better target to hit than the jaw.

To hit in the area of the ear, the suspect's head needs to be turned so that you punch at his profile. It's important that your blow is delivered on a straight line so that your two big knuckles make contact. I also show with pictures in *Anything Goes* that if your hand is angled even a little, you risk spraining or breaking it. That is why hitting the head is always a risk, even for a veteran karate fighter. The head can change angles ever so slightly at the last second, causing the fist to land on an uneven surface.

The bottom line is this: when you punch someone in the

head, you risk making the cast man at your local hospital emergency room just a little bit richer.

The Palm Heel

You significantly reduce the risk of injuring your hand when you hit with your palm heel. Do this: hold your arm out in front of you and bend your hand back as if you were going to palm open a door. Notice how beefy your palm is and how unbeefy your knuckles are, and how your palm is in alignment and supported by your forearm, and that your forearm is supported by your upper arm, which is supported by your shoulder. The fist easily flexes and pivots and must be perfectly aligned so that impact is absorbed by the two large knuckles. The palm heel, though, hits solidly with little flexing or pivoting. You can't ask for much more than that. It's as if God wanted you to hit people with your palm.

Some people like to deliver the palm-heel strike with their fingers open, while others like to curl them in. I prefer to curl mine, since I have long fingers and I want to get them out of the way. I also find that it makes my hand harder (in my young and stupid days, I used to break cinder blocks with a palm-heel strike).

This book is not about the mechanics of technique, so I am not going to go into anymore detail about the palm-heel strike. I encourage you, however, to look elsewhere to learn the many intricacies of how to deliver it as well as other hand blows.

Hitting to "Open the Door"

A citizen can hit in self-defense and then run away. But if the situation requires that you hit in your role as a police officer, you have to stay at the scene and get control of the suspect. That's what you get the big bucks for.

The question often debated in fighting circles is this: should your first blow be a power one, or should it be a fast one? The answer: although many fighters hold the false belief that it's best to use power first, enlightened fighters know that it's much more effective to first hit with speed. Hit quick as a blink, then overwhelm the suspect with your power. Think of it this way: speed opens the door for your power.

When I use the baton, I like to lead with a quick strike to the suspect's hands to give him a taste of acute pain. This usually forces him to focus his attention on his throbbing fingers, which gives me a second or two to deliver a baton thrust to his midsection. If I'm empty-handed, I like to pop a quick knuckle strike to the back of a suspect's hand, for the same reasons as with the baton, and then move in quickly and apply a control hold. Whether with the baton or my empty hands, my quick move opens the door so that once I'm inside, I can use a power move in some fashion to gain control.

Palm-Heel Strike to Distract

One of the problems with trying to do jujitsu on violent suspects in police work is that you are limited in how far you can go to distract a suspect before you do a technique. In my martial arts school, we precede most of our grappling techniques with a distraction hit of some kind (we call it "softening"), and sometimes we hit in the middle of a control hold if our opponent starts to stiffen up or fight back.

The nature of police work does not always allow for that option. When you grab a suspect by his arm and he tenses up, your agency just doesn't cotton to your slapping the guy's face, punching his throat, or grabbing a handful of his groin and squeezing before you apply an elbow lock. The suspect, your administration, the media, and every bleeding-heart cop watcher would have a festival hanging you out to dry. Being unable to execute a softening technique in most resist situations can make the application of a control hold difficult. However, if a situation is serious enough, meaning that your safety or another person's safety is at risk, you are justified to hit to distract to "open the door" for a control hold.

One time a wino tried to hit me with a bottle. I managed to sidestep his attack, foot sweep him, and take him down onto his back. He landed clutching the bottle to his chest and then partially curled himself into a fetal position as he screamed police brutality. I tried to get the bottle from him, but he held on to it with a death grip that even the fire department's "jaws of life" couldn't have pried loose. Because he had already shown that he was a threat with the bottle and had no intention of releasing it, I gave him a sharp palm-heel strike to the groin. He yelped, released his grip on the bottle, and grabbed desperately at his throbbing cookies. I tossed the bottle behind me and then easily rolled him over and slapped on the cuffs.

I categorize "hitting to distract" techniques as those delivered in situations where you need to divert a suspect's mind so you can apply a control hold. They are not life-and-death situations (although you never know) but are nonetheless serious enough that you have to take swift action to prevent a serious situation from becoming even more serious. Generally, the situation would not require full-power blows, but rather medium-power ones delivered to divert the suspect's thought process.

Palm-Heel Strike to Hurt

My partner and I were walking through a 100-yard stretch of eight-foot-high hedges that bordered the I-405 freeway in Portland. Sixty feet below the sloped embankment, busy commuters rolled past, unaware of the community of transients that lived in the shrubbery. We had been making our way through the underbrush for several minutes when we came upon a couple having sex: a woman giving a man a little early afternoon delight.

Actually, it really wasn't a woman. I'd known Yolanda for several years as a skidrow regular, a male prostitute with breast implants, though he still hung on to his male plumbing (so to speak). Whenever Yolanda drank all his/her money away and couldn't afford his/her hormone shots for the month, a telltale beard would poke through his/her heavy makeup. So if you were a skidrow bum and had a daily .18 blood alcohol level, you would be blind to all of Yolanda's little flaws and just might think he/she looked pretty darn good.

Anyway, Yolanda continued to service the guy for about a full minute after we walked up, oblivious that we were standing there watching like a couple of porno theater voyeurs. Finally, I broke the ice and asked, "So, what's up?" Both jumped a foot and then scrambled to their feet, the trick's pants still bunched around his ankles. He started to bad-mouth me, partly out of embarrassment and partly out of frustration, since his rocket had been about ready to launch. It was then that I pointed out, with sadistic pleasure, that his date was really a guy.

You can imagine his anger at this little piece of information. He didn't take it out on Yolanda, though; he took it out on the bearer of the bad news—me. And since I was having such a good time listening to the guy's verbal tirade at me, my guard was down, and my reflexes were taking a siesta. Before I could react, the angry trick grabbed a heavy tree limb hanging to the side of us and snapped it into my face.

It hurt, but it pissed me off more. Without thought, I thrust out a fast palm-heel and caught him in the forehead, snapping his head back. He slammed against Yolanda, who had been standing there quiet as a lamb and probably wondering if he/she was going to get his/her five bucks out of the guy. They both toppled over the embankment.

Imagine this for a moment. You and your family are driving along I-405 when out of the blue you see an odd-looking couple—a guy naked from the waist down entangled with another person, a weird-looking person—tumbling toward you, asshole over teakettle down the steep, litter-strewn embankment.

Now, I'm not going to try to justify my palm-heel strike in that situation. My point in telling it is to illustrate its powerful potential. The technique was not delivered with maximum power, but it still did a good job. Of course, the 60-foot embankment helped a little.

Here is a list of targets that cause excruciating pain when struck with a palm-heel strike:

1. *Nose.* No, you are not going to drive the nose bone into the brain—that nonsense is an old wive's tale. There is, however, good and bad about hitting a suspect in the nose. First the good.

The nose has many sensitive nerves and because of its placement (between the eyes on most folks), the nerves are closely associated with the eyes. Even a light blow to the snot box can cause excruciating pain, immediate watering of the eyes, and temporary blindness. And, as I said elsewhere in this book, if your opponent can't see, he ain't worth a damn in a fight.

The nose is an easy target to hit since it protrudes from the face (mine really protrudes) and can be struck with an upward, downward, straight, from

A palm-heel to the forehead is disorienting and creates a distraction for a follow-up technique.

left to right, or from right to left direction of force.

The bad news is that the nose has lots of blood vessels, so when it's struck hard, it will probably bleed a river. In fact, it often bleeds far worse than the severity of the blow justifies, and when it happens, you can be guaranteed that there will be a tourist nearby capturing the moment on video. But if the situation justifies such a strike, don't hesitate to do what needs to be done.

2. *Forehead.* A blow to the forehead can cause shock and be quite disorienting. The suspect often feels in his mind that he is going over backwards, which opens the door for you to follow up with another technique to take him all the way over onto his back.

3. *Jaw.* A hard blow anywhere against the jawbone causes a tremendous jarring effect and a sense that the jaw is broken.

4. *Back of the head.* A palm-heel strike to the lower back of the

head, called the brain stem, causes an acute jarring sensation, dizziness, loss of balance, and disorientation.

5. *Ear.* A blow to the ear has much the same effect as a blow to the back of the head. In addition, the suspect will hear a loud explosion upon impact, a result of shock to the eardrum.

6. *Throat.* A blow to the Adam's apple will drop even the biggest, toughest hombre and convince him that he has a Volkswagen caught in his throat. It's a horrible feeling that often lasts for days.

7. *Back and side of the neck.* This causes the same grief as a blow to the back of the head or the ear.

8. *Front of the shoulder.* This doesn't hurt much, but it's a good device to spin a suspect around.

9. *Upper chest.* This may or may not hurt the suspect, depending on his tolerance and the amount of force used. However, it often shocks him long enough to give you time to flow into your next move. If the suspect's body is angled slightly back when you hit him in the chest, the blow will probably knock him backwards.

10. *Solar plexus.* This target, located just below the pectorals, houses many nerves. A hard blow there can be debilitating.

11. *Kidney.* A hard strike to the kidney can be as debilitating as a hit in the groin.

12. *Groin.* While this is the absolute worst for most people, you should know that it doesn't work on everyone. Muhammad Ali could take a full hit there without flinching, and I've seen a few martial artists who could withstand a full power kick to the cookies. Most often, though, the suspect will drop into the fetal position and spray the sidewalk with his last cheeseburger.

13. *Legs.* Although you can deliver powerful kicks to several places on a suspect's leg to debilitate him, inside the thigh is the best target for the palm-heel strike, which is a weaker technique than a kick. Say you have fallen onto one knee and the suspect moves toward you to finish you off. Wait until he has his full weight on the leg that's closer to you and then drive your palm into his inner thigh. This hurts, and it might even buckle his leg.

When the suspect moves in on the downed officer, the officer covers his face and drives a palm-heel into the tender area of the suspect's inner thigh, slightly above his knee.

Blows to these targets hurt worse when the target is supported by a wall or the floor. For example, when the suspect is squirming on his back and the outside of one of his legs is touching the floor, he is in a prime position for you to strike inside his thigh. Since the floor will prevent his leg from giving, all of the energy from the palm-heel will go straight into his thigh, causing intense pain and momentary debilitation.

The palm-heel strike is a good technique to use against a suspect's head and body. Compared to hitting with the fist, there is less chance you are going to injure your hand with the palm-heel strike, and the technique is more acceptable to a critical citizenry.

Punching with the Fist

We talked about punching the head earlier, but, as we discussed, the body is a softer target, so there is less risk to your hand than when hitting a rock-hard skull.

As with the palm-heel, you can punch the throat (which is

A strong sidefist to the sternum will leave the suspect gasping.

potentially lethal, so make sure you are justified), chest, abdomen, and groin. Perhaps the two best targets for stopping or stunning a suspect are the ribs and the sternum, between the pectorals. Unless you are trained, however, there is still a risk of hurting your wrist if you hit wrong. So, let's examine how you should form your fist.

Sidefist

Boxers shoot their fists straight out with little, if any, rotation, generally with the palm side facing down. Karate fighters rotate their fist, usually beginning with the palm side facing up and then rotating the fist in a snapping motion as it travels to the target, or sometimes twisting it on the target. Both types of fighters, no matter how well trained, will still break their hand from time to time.

Let's look at a punch called a "sidefist," which will considerably reduce the risk of injury. Here is how you do it.

Stand with your left leg forward and hold your right hand near your solar plexus. Step forward toward the target with your left foot and thrust your right fist out, thumb-side up. Hit the target and then snap your arm back. It's as simple as that.

By not rotating your fist to the palm-down position, your elbow stays tucked in and pointed at the floor, as opposed to pointed off to the side when you rotate your wrist over. When your elbow is pointed down, you get a better bone alignment from your knuckles to your shoulder. In addition, your fist is less flexible and less likely to get sprained. Always aim with your index and middle knuckle.

Hitting with the Lead Hand

When you stand in the interview position, say with your left leg forward and your gun side to the rear, your left hand becomes your lead hand, therefore, your closer hand. It's not your strongest weapon, because the rest of your body isn't involved much in its delivery, but it's your quickest because it has less distance to travel to the target. Your rear hand is your most powerful because it has to travel a greater distance to the target, which means it builds more energy and momentum and incorporates more body involvement.

Since your lead hand is your faster one, it should be your first choice when you need to hit with the element of surprise. With a little practice, you can hit a suspect virtually without telegraphing your move. Using your palm-heel strike, for example, you can thrust it into a suspect's face, chest, or solar plexus easily and quickly from the classic police interview position.

The function of the lead-hand strike is not to knock out your suspect (although if you do, all your buddies in the locker room will be talking about you for months). Your objective is to deliver a fast strike to shock the suspect enough to stop his aggression or to distract him so you can more easily apply a control hold.

Say a suspect is verbally threatening you and positioning himself to throw a punch or a kick. Although this may be a situation for your baton, you left it in your car (shame on you), and you can't draw your firearm because you are in a crowded bar. Since you have developed a philosophy that you don't get paid enough to let someone swing at you first, you decide to defend yourself offensively by beating the suspect—to the punch, that is. Your hands should already be raised, since that places you in a quick reactionary position. As fast as you can without winding it up, thrust your palm-heel straight out and slam it into the suspect's chest. Then, as he staggers back a step, eyes bulging with surprise, you rush in and apply a takedown technique with enough vigor to bury the creep in the sidewalk.

Here is another situation. This time let's say you are in the middle of a domestic dispute, a big nasty fight between a husband and wife. You thought you had them separated, but as you talk with the female, the husband steps around you and lifts his arms toward his wife as if to choke her. Wham! Your lead hand snaps out, and your palm thumps against the husband's shoulder, catching him off balance. You move in, get him controlled, and slap on the handcuffs.

Vulnerable Targets for the Lead Hand

If your safety is in danger, you are justified to use extreme measures to survive. The eyes and the throat are excellent targets that will weaken the strongest suspects and buy you a little time to follow up with another blow, a control technique, or to retreat and wait for reinforcements. The lead hand is perfect for striking these vulnerable targets because it's so close, at least half again as close as your rear hand.

Eyes

Poking your fingers into a suspect's eyes may sound extreme for police work, but if the situation is serious enough and you can articulate the need for such severe measures, then go for it. John Wayne, Chuck Norris, and Arnold Schwarzenegger may be tough men, but a poke in the eye from a little finger will bring them down in a second. You don't need much power for an eye poke; all you have to do is just flick your lead hand out quick as a blink (pun intended).

The best way to hold your hand is to spread all five of your fingers as if you were trying to palm a large ball and then thrust your hand toward the suspect's face. When you poke with all five

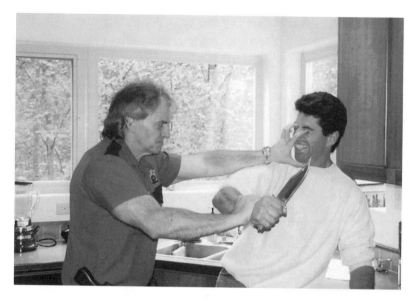

The officer jams the suspect's knife arm against his chest and then thrusts his fingers into the man's eyes.

fingers, you greatly increase your chance of hitting the suspect's little beady eyes. You can also rake the suspect's eyes using the same hand configuration. Simply rake it across his eyes from left to right or right to left. There is no penetration with this method, and you are using all five fingers, which gives you five chances to get the target.

Throat

Punching the front of the throat will drop a big guy, too. It's a horrible sensation to get struck in the front of the throat, and I can tell you from experience (I was the recipient of a spinning back kick there once) that the suspect will be convinced he is going to die. Use your sidefist and thrust it out like a boxer's jab. The throat is a soft target, so even if your fist doesn't land right, it's still going to hurt him more than it's going to hurt you.

Don't think of your lead-hand blow as the only technique you will do. Instead, consider it a shock technique, one used to "open the door" to a follow-up technique, such as any of the following.

- Hit, then step back and draw your baton, chemical spray, or your firearm.
- Hit, then rush forward and apply a control hold.
- Hit, then hit again.
- Hit, then move to a better location (such as when dealing with multiple opponents).
- Hit, then retreat a few steps and ask radio for backup.

Obviously, you have to be justified to hit a suspect, whether it's a mild strike (such as a palm-heel to the suspect's shoulder), or one of greater severity (such as five fingers into his eyes). Whether the administration or the community likes it or understands, there are definitely situations where hitting is justified. The administration is not going to think about it because they live and work where it's safe. But you are the one out there facing the dragon, so you need to think and visualize how you would use a technique like the lead-hand strike to survive a hairy situation.

Hitting with the Knee

Knee strikes are excellent close-range techniques. They can be delivered straight up or in a circular, roundhouse fashion. Straight knee strikes are easy to do because the motion is a natural one. On the other hand, circular knee strikes require training because they are not as natural.

Knee strikes work best when you can grab hold of the suspect, which makes them a good option if the suspect has hold of you and is pulling you in to him. You can grab his upper arms, chest, or, as Thai kickboxers do, circle one or both your arms around his neck and pull him in while you slam him with hard knee strikes.

Because you are hitting with your bony kneecap, you will cause pain anywhere you hit, whether it's in the groin, stomach, chest, or face. If the suspect is quick enough to cover himself with his arms, just hit his forearms with your knee strikes, and he will move them out of the way.

KICKING

Kicking is not recommended unless you are highly trained in the art of fighting with your feet. Jackie Chan and Jean Claude Van Damme make it look easy, and so do black belt karate fighters. But these people have spent years training for power, speed, precision, and—this is the big one—balance, since lifting a foot off the floor to kick means the kicker has to balance himself on one leg. This isn't easy if you are untrained, especially if you are trying to kick someone who is moving.

There are many karate students who are surprised to learn how precarious their balance is when they first kick a heavy bag. In some schools students spend several weeks, sometimes months, learning the intricacies of the front, back, side, and round kicks by practicing hundreds of repetitions in the air. Then one day the instructor introduces them to the heavy bag. Now those same kicks that looked so good in the air land on the bag with all the power of a pat from an aging bunny rabbit. Even when these new students do land a solid kick, more times than not, they lose their balance or land flat on their butts.

It's true that these problems are eventually overcome with training and good coaching. My point, though, is that the kicking skill necessary to stop, distract, or hurt a violent suspect doesn't come easily. It takes training. How much? Who knows? It depends on the quality of the training and the ability of the student to learn and physically apply his knowledge. For example, I've taught women's self-defense classes where after a couple hours, five students out of twenty were landing fairly hard blows on the kicking shield. Why did one-quarter of the class adapt quickly to the lesson while three-quarters did not? Perhaps those five were athletically inclined, or maybe they had trained previously in the martial arts. The other 15 students would have eventually kicked skillfully, too, but it would have taken considerably more time.

Most people don't learn to kick as quickly as they learn how to use their hands. When perfected, kicking techniques are awesome weapons that can bring a suspect down hard. But when you are not trained, or trained inadequately, using the feet for self-defense can be hazardous to your health. Even if you are a trained kicker, here are some considerations you need to think about.

Uniform Restrictions

Most uniform pants are form-fitting, meaning they are restrictive when it comes to throwing kicks to any target higher than the suspect's groin (more so if the suspect is an NBA player). When I was 19 years old, I got into a fight at a local burger joint. Early in the scrap, I kicked the guy in the face, ripping the butt and crotch out of my pants, giving me ventilation, embarrassment, and a warm round of applause from the crowd.

Often, I have seen officers rip out the seat of their pants, a result of eating too many doughnuts and wrestling with suspects in a way that stretched their pants beyond the limitation of the material. Uniform pants always give out at their weakest point, which is usually the seam in the crotch area. Something to think about.

Footwear

Some officers prefer to wear boots because they like their heaviness and the hard toes. Yes, you can kick with the hard toe, but the weight of the boot restricts the speed, height, and type of kick you can use.

It can also be hard on the knee joint. I learned in the army that when wearing heavy boots it was best to use kicks that relied on thrusting motions, as opposed to kicks that snap the knee joint. The first two times I popped a guy with a roundhouse kick while wearing Uncle Sam's 10-pound jump boots, I was left limping with a puffed-up knee. Thrusts kicks, on the other hand, come from driving the hips or pelvic area toward the target.

The best targets while wearing heavy boots are those that are low and vulnerable, such as the suspect's ankle, inner thigh, shin, and groin.

Many agencies allow uniformed officers to wear black, lightweight running shoes, such as Nike or adidas. These are great for kicking to higher targets and kicking with a variety of fast kicks.

However, because they have relatively soft toes, they are not appropriate for kicking the same way as you do with heavy boots.

Where to Kick

I'm going to limit the targets for kicking to just those below the waist. These are highly vulnerable places to hit and can be so painful that they not only disrupt a suspect's thinking process, but they can debilitate him from further aggression. After all, you don't bring a tree down by plucking at its leaves; you hack at the trunk. Save the fancy Jean Claude Van Damme kicks for the movies. Your job is to stop the suspect or bring him down quickly. For example, slamming the hard toe of a boot against a suspect's lower leg, anywhere from the knee to his ankle, will definitely get his attention. Since this area has very little protective meat around it and lots of sensitive nerves, a kick there causes intense, acute pain.

The Shin Area

Remember the last time you banged your shin into the bedpost in the middle of the night? The toe of a running shoe is too soft for that type of kick, but you can kick the edge of it into the suspect's shin or scrape it down the tender shinbone.

The Thigh

Outside and inside the thigh are good targets that, when hit hard enough with either a boot or running shoe, will often drop a suspect in a quick second. The peroneal nerve that runs down the outside of the thigh is extremely vulnerable to kicks and will cause a sympathetic reflex in the other leg, forcing both to buckle. The upper inside of the thigh is quite sensitive and the slight "pocket" inside the thigh next to the kneecap is vulnerable to a hard kick, which often causes the other leg to give out, too.

The Groin

Don't put all your nuts in one basket and count on a groin kick to drop a suspect. Sometimes it does, and sometimes it doesn't. It's also a hard target to hit, because guys, being guys, are quite protective of the area and get rather defensive when there is a threat to it. Of course, if you have a clean shot, go for it, but be on guard just in case the suspect is one of those people who are not affected by a solid groin kick.

Don't kick straight at the groin, but kick with the shoestring area of your boot or shoe, snapping your foot up. You want to slam the suspect's cookies against his pelvis area; better yet, against his chin.

How to Kick

If you are wearing boots, use the hard toe to kick targets below the suspect's groin, but use the bottom of your boot if you insist on kicking higher. Kicking with the toe to a target higher than the shin may injure your foot. It took me three sprained ankles in Vietnam to realize that it wasn't a good idea to kick with the ball or the toe of my army boot to a suspect's midsection. When I kicked with the bottom of my foot in a hard thrusting motion, I didn't get hurt (in *The Way of the Warrior*, published by Paladin, I relate how I accidentally kicked a prisoner out a second-story window with a front thrust kick).

If your running shoes are flexible enough, you can curl your toes up and kick with the ball of your foot when delivering a thrust kick. But when throwing a circular kick, you should hit with the shoestring portion.

Both the boot and the shoe can be launched in a sidekick fashion into a suspect's ankle, shin, and knee area.

Kicking with the Shins

Kicking with the shin is a good technique when the suspect is close to you. The action of the leg is the same as when you are kicking with your foot, but the impact area is your bony shin. Slam a hard shin kick straight up into a suspect's groin and the guy will follow you anywhere—once he gets back on his feet. Drive a circular shin kick into the side of his thigh and you will get his undivided attention.

Few martial artists or police officers consider kicking with the shinbone. They should because it's effective and it's one more weapon that can be used at close range. Try it on a bag; you will be surprised at how hard you can kick with it.

MASS ATTACK

There is nothing quite like the feeling of realizing you are surrounded by a bevy of assholes who want to make your plastic surgeon a little richer. Although Jackie Chan and Bruce Lee would have a blast in such a predicament, you are not one of these celluloid wonders. You just want to keep your undies as white as they were when you put them on this morning.

One night, I went into a tavern on a routine walk-through. It was a scummy beer joint in a scummy part of town that always attracted scummy beer guzzlers. I was about five feet into the place when I heard a distinctive metallic click behind me. I turned in time to see a beer-gutted, tattooed slob sliding the front-door dead bolt into place and smiling at me like he was looking at a dead man. Behind me I saw several beer mugs being set down and big butts sliding off barstools.

For certain, they weren't going to gather around and sing, "For he's a jolly good fellow," so I pulled my baton and stepped around the corner of the bar. The bar mirror was to my back and the bartender (also an asshole) was at the far end, so I wasn't worried about him. I was concerned about the other six or seven guys moving my way like wolves toward a stray chicken.

The bozo who locked the door was still standing by it, blocking my escape route, so I whipped my baton into his shoulder, knocking the smile off his mug and his body into a couple of his buddies, which momentarily blocked their way. I then drove my shoulder into the next closest guy and pushed him into two others behind him. I had created a window of opportunity to get my rear out of there, so I seized the moment and did just that.

That incident happened early in my career, and there have been many others over the years. Here are three more off the top of my head.

- President Bush visited Portland frequently during his administration, and each time there were mass demonstrations in the street; so many and so intense that the

Secret Service labeled Portland, "Little Beirut." There were several demonstrations where the 200 officers we had assigned to them were not enough, and they had to fight in a frenzy of baton strikes, wristlocks, kicks, and punches. I did a knee drop on the face of a guy who had seconds earlier attempted to tackle me, and I still remember (with some degree of pleasure) the sickening sound of his cheekbone cracking.

- I recall an incident when three of us were trapped at the top of an embankment underneath a freeway overpass as 75 to 100 protesters rushed up the hill. We sprayed pepper, swung our batons, and punched chests as we endured a deluge of bricks, rocks, and bottles.
- There were several occasions when we had to go into a high school brawl that involved hundreds of rival high-school football fans. We were pushed, punched, and kicked; and we had our cars rocked back and forth and our prisoners pulled away from us as we fought tooth and nail with 17- and 18-year-olds.

I can think of at least a dozen more incidents, but you get the idea. A mass attack can happen in a variety of situations and so quickly and unexpectedly that you have little or no time to think about it. Therefore, it's important to think about it now and experiment with it in your training.

Let's take a look at several things to consider when dealing with a mass attack. The precise techniques I'll leave to you and your study.

1. *You must think quickly and anticipate the attackers' moves.*
2. *Think in terms of striking targets that either stun or are potentially lethal.* Consider striking the temple, throat, mastoid, spine, solar plexus, kidneys, groin, and knees. These targets maximize the effectiveness of your blows, thus conserving your strength and energy.
3. *You must control your breathing to keep your anxiety in check and your energy level high.*

4. *Move fluidly with grace and balance.*
5. *Power can be increased by adding leverage, speed of delivery, and mass.* Leverage points are usually fixed joints, such as elbows, wrists, knees, and shoulders. Application of strikes or blows to these leverage points can take the suspect down and cause excruciating pain. The greater the speed of the technique, the greater the power. The use of your leg, as opposed to your arm, will add mass to a leverage technique. For example, sweeping your leg against a suspect's leg has greater power and leverage than pressing your forearm against his elbow.
6. *If you are fighting with your hands, be careful not to injure them.* If you have a strong punch, you might have a tendency to overuse it and risk injury. Choose soft targets to hit that are vulnerable, yet aren't likely to injure you, as will hitting hard targets.

Marc "Animal" MacYoung, author of *Street E&E: Evading, Escaping, and Other Ways to Save Your Ass When Things Get Ugly* and several other books available from Paladin Press, provided me with the following suggestions for surviving a mass attack:

> *Generally, when you are up against a mass attack, there are only a few people really committed. The rest will jump in after the risk is reduced by others who pile on to you first. If you drop the instigators fast and brutally so the others can see it, it tends to reduce the others' desire to get involved. The weaker ones rely on numbers and the fact that their tougher friends are out front to keep them safe. If you drop the tough ones, the weaker ones realize they shouldn't get involved.*

MacYoung said that he likes to make the "mouth" solely accountable. For example, he will tell the vocal one that his friends might get him in a rush, but he is going to make the vocal one's "head into a canoe." This holds the vocal one responsible for whatever follows.

"Triangles are bad," MacYoung says about strategy. "When you are talking about two against one, a triangle is formed when the three of you are not in a straight line. Try to keep the line, which means you have to move around to keep one attacker in front of the other. This makes them trip and fall all over each other as they try to get you.

"Stay moving," MacYoung advises, drawing on his years of experience as a bouncer. "When you stay in one place, the others in the attack may not know what is going on. But when you punch a hole—that is, take out one guy—then move, the rest of the group will have to stop and reorient, especially if the one you took out is their leader. This gives you time to strategically withdraw to a better location (translation: get your ass out of there)."

DEFENDING AGAINST A GUN

There is an awesome amount of crap written on how to defend against a gun. Facing a weapon is not a time for flippy-dippy kicks and other fancy-schmancy moves. Nor should you only think about jamming a semiautomatic's slide or gripping the cylinder on a revolver. These moves are too finite and, besides, the shooter can still get one round off, anyway. When you are facing a razor-sharp weapon is not the time to get fancy.

Wristlocks are risky because they usually require two hands, leaving you defenseless against an attack from the suspect's free hand. Besides, unless you are a highly trained martial artist, wristlocks are also finite and difficult to apply when you are scared shitless. In addition, thinking too much about a wristlock on the gun hand, prevents you from thinking about the real danger of the weapon—that little projectile that explodes out the end.

It takes very little motion and effort for the suspect to pull the trigger, and, if in the act of applying a cool wristlock you have not moved that barrel aside or your body out of the way, you are in big trouble. Another problem is that if he has a two-handed grip on the gun a wristlock is difficult, if not impossible, to apply in such an extreme situation. Or, if he is gripping the gun with one hand and you zero in on his wrist, there is nothing to prevent him from simply grabbing the weapon with his free hand.

I am going to leave the specific techniques up to your wisdom. However, let me lay out some basic concepts and principles that should be part of whatever techniques you apply.

1. *If you and the gunman are 10 feet apart, do whatever he says and try to talk to him.* Try to distract him with a little begging and beseeching, maybe telling him a sad story about how your kid needs a prosthetic leg. My point is that being 10 feet from the suspect is too far to do anything other than verbalize. If you are convinced he is going to shoot, keep him talking and work your way closer to him.

2. *Another option when the gunman is more than 10 feet away is to turn and run like hell.* Statistics confirm a low hit rate when a gunman is firing at a running target, and, contrary to Western movies, experts say that running in a zigzag doesn't increase the miss rate. They recommend that you just run as fast as you are able.

3. *If you are a step away from the gunman, or closer, your odds are better.* However, you want to remember two of the principles discussed in Chapter 2: the action/reaction principle, which says action is faster than reaction, and the distraction principle, which says a person can only think of one thing at a time. One of the best "tricks" that relates to both principles is to talk to the gunman or get him to talk. Talking occupies his brain with having to listen to you or with having to think about what he is saying. When you make your move, he has to stop his brain in order to react to what you are doing. This mental switch doesn't take long, so you have to move fast.

4. *The element of surprise is of upmost importance.* Explode with all the speed you can muster and do not telegraph your intentions.

5. *Remove yourself from the path of the bullet.* (Did I really have to tell you to do that?) This is done by moving the suspect's gun hand and moving your body. If you can do both simul-

Be careful when knocking a rifle barrel away that you don't get rewarded with a butt stroke to the chops.

taneously, such as deflecting the gun arm across the suspect's body while twisting your waist, you increase your odds of being alive to tell the story later.

6. *The type of parry you use is based on where your arms are when you move.* Are they down at your sides, up in the air, or behind your head?

7. *If you are a step or two away from a right-handed suspect, step diagonally to your left as you knock his arm across his body.*

8. *Knock his arm across his body.* This positions you to his backside away from his free hand, which makes it difficult, if not impossible, for him to hit you. Additionally, most shooters are more accurate with a gun when they move their arm across their body, as opposed to moving it to the outside of their body. This is good for you, since you are positioned to the outside.

9. *Trap or neutralize the weapon without applying a wristlock.* One way is to press your attacker's gun hand against his body.

10. *Keep pressing his gun arm against his body and attack him with your free hand.* Gouge his eyes and punch his throat. Don't stop to admire your work. Keep hitting and gouging until he is no longer a threat and you have his weapon in your hand.

11. *If he is holding a rifle on you, deflect the barrel since his hands are too far away to deflect.* Be careful when you step in diagonally that he doesn't pop you with the rifle butt.

DEFENDING AGAINST THE BLADE

I don't have statistics to support this, but it certainly seems that there are more knives on the street now than ever. Calibre Press, one of the leading training organizations for law enforcement officers, says that in the past 10 years, injuries to officers from knife attacks have increased more than 90 percent. For sure, everyone and their brother carries a folding knife, some of which are the size of an overgrown zucchini, and every other street person has a fixed blade in a sheath, which usually dangles from the hips to the knees.

If it's not a blade in the pocket or on the hip, it's a hypodermic needle, usually uncapped and easily accessible from the shirt pocket or the elastic of a sock. You are always concerned about getting pricked by a needle and catching who-knows-what kind of disease, but you must also keep in mind that a needle can be used to stab you just as easily as a Gerber.

It seems there are as many knife fighting styles as there are knife fighters, and it's this variety of possibilities that makes training for knife defense far more difficult than training to defend against a gun. One knife fighter will hold his knife in his lead hand, another fighter will hold it in his rear hand, another behind his back, and others will hold it to their front and make continuous jabbing motions with it. Knife fighters use a variety of grips, too, some holding it by the blade and some by the handle. There are fighters who like to slash, and there are those who like to stab. One guy will swing at you from arm's reach, and another will wait until he is literally on top of you and gut punch you with it. Some fighters favor cute little knives and others like big ugly ones.

Knife fighters who spend a lot of time perfecting their knife-fighting skills are mostly found among martial artists, prisoners, street gangsters, and people whose cultures emphasize fighting with a knife. There is still another group of people we need to be concerned about because their numbers are growing at an alarming rate, especially in the inner cities. I'm referring to the mentally disturbed and transient/homeless people. The mentally disturbed folks carry knives because they are paranoid, and transients carry them because of a need for protection in the dangerous world of the street. These people may not spend any time honing their fighting skills, but they are typically in possession of some kind of a bladed weapon.

What all this means to you is that there is a large variety of dangerous people carrying knives, some of whom are highly skilled in a variety of fighting styles and some of whom are not. But whether a blade is wielded by a master or a stupid drunk, it can still cut you, and cut you badly. Even if it's flailed haphazardly, it can sever an artery or, as your mother use to warn, take out an eye.

There is a lot of silliness in books and magazines about how to defend against a knife attack. Actually, *scary* is a better word than *silly*, because the crap some of these writers come up with is more ridiculous than a Jackie Chan movie and dangerous to anyone who would take this misinformation seriously. Flippy-dippy kicks and jumping this-and-that are excellent techniques with which to commit suicide when facing even an untrained suspect with a knife.

Knife Defense Techniques
Now, I'm not one of those guys who says that if you haven't faced a blade in a real situation you don't have anything intelligent to offer on the subject. I have wrestled with a suspect armed with a knife, and the experience didn't make me any better at it than I was before. I believe that a martial artist who is analytical and wise to the ways of the street, though he may have never faced a real knife con-

frontation, is quite capable of developing sound defensive techniques as long as they are based on realistic concepts. When researching defense techniques to use against the knife, it's important that you keep them simple. It doesn't matter if you are learning from an experienced knife fighter, a high-ranking martial artist, or a how-to-do book or video. What is absolutely mandatory is that you maintain a theme of simplicity. When you are facing a razor-sharp weapon is no time to get fancy.

Things to Keep in Mind Before You Confront a Blade
Here are important knife fighting concepts that your defense should include:

1. *Accept mentally that you will probably get cut.* Statistics say that there is a one-in-three chance you will get cut when defending against a blade. No matter how good you are and no matter whether you practice defending against a knife your entire life, your wrists, forearms, and fingers most likely will get hacked because they are used in your blocks and grabs. It's paramount, however, that you do everything you can to not get stabbed. There is a big difference between getting stabbed and getting cut. For example, you will probably be able to continue to fight when your shoulder has been sliced open, but there are many body targets that are lethal when stabbed and penetrated only one inch.

2. *Accept that a knife attack can happen anytime and anywhere.* We are in the era of Uzis, Glocks, MAC-11s, and a whole assortment of other mystical guns. Although weapon technology has progressed rapidly over the past 10 years, knives are more prevalent now than ever. They are carried in pockets, backpacks, purses, and under car seats. The ease of their concealability means that you must keep in the forefront of your mind the fact that a knife assault can happen under any circumstances and anywhere. Officers who have faced the cold steel report that they were surprised when the suspect attacked them with a knife because it was the furthest thing from their thoughts.

Many officers say they would shoot a knife attacker. The problem is that you may never get the chance because most attacks happen so suddenly and at such a close range that the only option is empty-hand defense. Remember, most knife attacks are going to happen when the suspect is literally on top of you. Yes, shooting is an excellent way to solve a knife attack, but the reality is that most of the time you are going to have to fight empty-handed before you get the opportunity to pop some rounds.

3. *Vests don't always help.* A buddy of mine was searching a woman when out of the blue a knife appeared in her hand, which she swung back and into his thigh. His vest didn't help. Other officers have reported that their vests stopped slashes but not stabs. Tonto brand knives used to be advertised in magazines as capable of penetrating police vests. As a result of write-in complaints the magazines stopped the ads, but nonetheless the knives are still out there and they still penetrate vests.

Things to Do After You See the Blade

1. *Never kick the blade.* A martial artist I know was jumped by an assailant armed with a knife. My friend launched a kung fu kick at the blade only to have the attacker do a fillet on his ankle, calf, and thigh before he could retract his foot. A hand holding a knife is too fast to kick.

2. *Don't fight the suspect toe-to-toe.* Continually sidestep the attacker or step in a 45-degree angle away from the trajectory of his blade, so he has to turn toward you. This gives you a little more time to deliver blows to his throat and eyes.

3. *Capture the suspect's attacking arm and control it.* There are different schools of thought as to the ideal place to grab the attacking arm. Some experts recommend the wrist, whereas others say to grab up higher near the elbow. You should experiment to see which you prefer. If I am pushing the arm away rather than grabbing it, I like to push near the elbow because the midarm leverage point makes for a stronger

push. But when grabbing, I just take whatever I can get, realizing that the knife hand still has considerable flexibility wherever it's grabbed. When I fought the knife-wielding suspect I mentioned earlier, I grabbed his hand, which was fisted around the handle of his knife. I held it away from me, sucked in my stomach and chest, and rotated his hand seemingly a couple of revolutions in a sankayjo hold until his screams deafened me and the blade dropped to the floor (I wanted to kick the crap out of him after that, but we were in a crowded shopping mall).

Be careful when taking a knife-wielding suspect down onto his back that he doesn't cut you on the way. Try to take him down face first.

4. *Blend with his attacking arm.* If the energy of his thrust carries him forward, step sideways or diagonally and pull him by you, or spin him around past you in a circle. If you grab his arm and he retracts it, hold on and let him pull you into him. After you have stopped flowing with his energy, hit him as hard and often as you can with your free hand. Don't let go of his knife hand.

5. *Strike his throat and eyes.* These are vulnerable targets that require very little force to injure and debilitate. Hit them as many times as it takes to get him to drop his weapon.

6. *Dump him onto the ground as hard as you can.* The idea is to shock the hell out of him, especially if his brain stem hits first. Marc MacYoung recommends that you drop him onto his back only if you have control of his knife arm. This is because when the knife arm is free as he falls backwards, he may flail

at you and intentionally or unintentionally cut you. He may also try to grab you for support with his knife hand and intentionally or unintentionally cut you. But when you take him down onto his belly, you reduce his ability to kick at you or swing the knife. And—oops!—he might even fall on it.

7. *Create distance and draw your weapon.* If your blows to his eyes and throat loosen his grip enough for you to get his blade, back off and draw your weapon. Or if your blows debilitate him enough to take the fight out of him, and for whatever reason taking him down is not an option, quickly back off and draw your weapon.

When backing away, avoid back pedaling in a straight line. It's too easy for the suspect to give chase and too easy for you to fall down. Instead, move off at an angle so that he has to turn and move toward you, which will give you a little additional time to unholster your weapon.

If for whatever reason you don't grab the suspect's arm, then sweep it away, create distance, and draw your weapon. If you have the opportunity, get an obstacle between you, such as a parking meter, mailbox, or car fender.

There are many variables in a knife assault. A frequently heard quotation from knife fighting experts is: "A knife fighter would never do this," or, "A knife assailant would never attack with this technique." This is nonsense. Knife assailants are made up of all kinds of people. In my 29 years of experience working around assholes with blades, not one of them was a skilled fighter. Some were drunks, some were mentally disturbed, some were simply assholes with knives. None of them showed any particular skill with their weapons. What this means to me is that when I practice knife defense, I practice against all kinds of attacks: wild and crazy flailings and clean, sophisticated movements.

This is worth repeating. Never say, and never listen to anyone who says, "An attacker with a knife would never do this." You don't know what an attacker, armed or unarmed, will do. Never rule out anything in a fight. Get the point? Good luck.

GROUND FIGHTING

Here is an oft-quoted statistic that I've always wondered about: "Ninety percent of all fights end up on the ground."

Really?

Now, I've been in three or four fights on the job, three or four hundred, that is. Probably more. Hey, who has time to count when you are having a good time? Some were big, hairy, knock-down-drag-outs, and others were minor skirmishes. After thinking about all of them, this is where I am confused about that 90 percent statistic: not one of my fights has gone to the ground. For sure, I have taken many people to the ground, some with extreme prejudice, but never did I go down with them when I didn't want to. I always followed up a takedown technique with a restraint hold, but I never rolled around on the ground with them in a wrestling match.

Is this because I am such a bad dude? No way—I'm a lover. Have I just been lucky? Since I wasn't sure, I asked several officers about their experiences, guys I know to be aggressive street officers who have had more than their share of street fights with suspects who didn't want to go to jail. Without knowing why I was asking, every one of them answered that they had never rolled around on the ground with a suspect. Yes, they had taken suspects to the ground, but they were able to restrain them with defensive tactics or just plain muscle power. I do know a few officers who have fought with suspects on the ground and, in fact, some have gotten injured doing it. The few who have, however, no way adds up to the 90 percent statistic.

Keep this thought in mind: statistics are just that, statistics, and we shouldn't get carried away with them. (My favorite is the one that says that 99 percent of all juvenile delinquents eat tomatoes. So?)

Every time I have heard this 90 percent quote (sometimes it's been 95 percent) about fights ending on the ground, it has been from a writer validating his article on ground fighting or an instructor hyping his ground fighting seminar. Think about it for a moment: who did the survey that resulted in this 90–95 percent number? And how did they do it? The answer is this: no one did. Someone just came up with the number, and everyone has since jumped on the bandwagon. So should we then ignore ground fighting defensive tactics? Of course not. Even if the number is 25 percent, which I would bet is closer to the truth, it's still important to include ground fighting techniques and concepts in your training.

Rolling around on the ground is extraordinarily dangerous for any fighter, more so for a police officer. Even on your feet, there is always an inherent risk of losing your firearm to a determined, combative suspect, and your risk of losing it on the ground is greater. Even if you are a highly skilled ground fighter, it's dangerous at best to fight with an uncontrolled law breaker on the concrete. Hey, concrete hurts.

I encourage you to explore ground fighting skills with a qualified teacher. In recent years there has been a plethora of ground fighting schools and seminars springing up around the country, and many of them can be found on your agency's teletype. If your defensive tactics program doesn't teach at least one or two techniques for getting a suspect off you when you are on your back, or one or two ways to immobilize a suspect once you are on top of him, encourage your instructors to get with the program.

Let's examine some concepts, principles, and tips that should be applied to whatever ground fighting techniques you incorporate.

Because cops are a notoriously negative lot, let's begin with a few negatives that will affect your ground fighting. I mention these here because I think it's important for you to think about them and have a plan B to go to in the event they happen to you.

Precise Positioning

You can have a super-duper killer ground fighting technique that would make Bruce Lee green with envy, but if you can't get the suspect's arms, legs, head, or whatever in the right position for it, you simply can't apply it.

You Are Up Against a Big Ol' Farm Boy

Ever so often you will come up against a suspect who is so

big and strong that he can muscle out of your powerful ground technique—that is, if you can get him into it in the first place.

Gumbys

Extremely flexible people can sometimes tolerate pain compliance techniques because you are not able to find the lockpoint in their joint. I've applied wristlocks on a couple of people only to find that their wrists were so flexible that their palms touched their forearms.

Drugs, Booze, Rage, and Mental Illness

Some people under the influence of any one of these four conditions may not feel your techniques. I ran into a fifth condition once when an outlaw biker's code of conduct was to not exhibit pain. I had his arm behind his back and was applying more and more pain on a wristlock only to have the greaser taunt me with a smile. Finally, I cranked as hard as I could, and his wrist broke with a sickening crack as loud as a shot from a .22 rifle. He stopped smiling then, but he still didn't show any pain even as his hand flopped around uselessly.

Flailers

It can be difficult, if not impossible, to apply a control technique on a person flailing his arms and legs all around.

Fatigue

Wrestling around on the ground is extremely energy draining, more so when you are fighting for your self-preservation. It's tough even when you are in shape, but when you are in poor physical condition, you are going to poop out in just a few seconds.

If you have fought on the ground, you no doubt noticed that the above situations are quite common. So what can be done when one or more of them happen to you? If you were just wrestling around with a friend, you would try to grapple or tickle your way out of the situation, but if you are on the job and struggling with a desperate suspect, you need to consider more extreme measures.

When I run into one of these negatives, I hit. Hitting softens the suspect and makes him amenable to the techniques I am trying to apply. Thrashing about on the sidewalk with someone who is not responding to your techniques for whatever reason is not a time for community policing or tricky psychology. It's a time to hit the bastard.

OK, enough negatives. Here are some positive tips, concepts, and principles that you should throw in with your ground fighting techniques.

Know When It's Inevitable That You Are Going to the Ground

Marc MacYoung says that most people struggle to stay upright too long after their body has been pushed past the point of no return. They get hurt because they try to stay upright instead of preparing themselves physically and mentally to hit the ground. When they do hit mother Earth, they aren't prepared tactically. He advises that when it's inevitable that you are going down, try to make it worse for the suspect than it is for you.

Land on the Suspect

When it's apparent that you are falling, keep hold of the suspect and land on top of him with one or both of your knees. The shock of hitting the ground and the penetrating impact from your knees will hurt him and, you hope, take the fight out of him.

Stay in Control of Yourself

Unless you practice ground fighting two or three times a week, suddenly finding yourself on the hard, cold cement can be a little intimidating. Nonetheless, you must stay in control of your mind so that you don't overreact or allow the suspect to get control of you physically. Concentrate on what you need to do to dominate the suspect, and get him into a position where you can control him.

Know Two Versatile Control Techniques

Have in your repertoire two strong techniques that you can use in a variety of situations on the ground. Understand how they work when you are in control of the suspect and how they work when the suspect is beginning to dominate you.

Go to the Suspect's Vulnerable Targets

If the suspect should start to dominate you on the ground, you must strike quickly because you are always at risk of losing your weapon. Strike at the suspect's eyes, throat, nose, and groin (in that order, if you

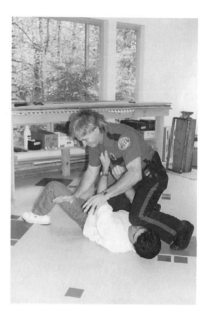

If the suspect pulls you down with him, try to land on him with your knees.

have a choice), targets that are vulnerable no matter what his size. Understand that if the suspect is dominating you, you are justified in striking these targets.

Keep Your Face and Head Area Covered

Your face is highly vulnerable to strikes when you are on the ground. Guard your face—especially your eyes and nose—and keep your head tucked into your shoulder.

Stay Off Your Stomach

The only thing good about being on your stomach is that you can't see what's hitting you. Everything else about the prone position is bad for you: you can't defend from it, you can be easily choked out, you can't counterattack, and you can't control or dominate the suspect when you are face down on the concrete.

You are vulnerable to just about anything when you are on your stomach.

Get Off Your Back as Soon as Possible

Yes, you have four weapons at your disposal when you are on your back, but you are not at your best in that position. As quickly as you can, get up into a squatting position where you can block, kick, and tackle. Then as quickly as you can, stand up.

Stay Off the Suspect's Hips

If for some reason you find yourself sitting on the suspect, stay off his hip area. It's easy for him to buck you off from this precarious position. Sit on his stomach or chest. The opposite is true if you end up on your back and he takes a seat on your hips. Simply bump your hips up and send him flying.

Watch Out for the Sucker Punch

Don't become a victim of tunnel vision so that when you have one of the suspect's arms controlled, you forget that he can still pummel you with his other.

Smother the Suspect's Flailing Arms

Say the suspect is on his back and is flailing his arms all around as he tries to block whatever you are doing and counter-strike you. From the outside of his body, press either of his arms across his chest. By pressing from the outside in, you reduce the chance of getting hit with his other arm.

Smack the Side of His Head to Turn Him Over

When the situation warrants it, such as when the suspect is connecting with hard blows to your head, use your palm to strike the side of his face. Your objective is to force him to turn away to avoid the smacks and eventually turn over onto his stomach. Even if he turns only part way, you are in a stronger position to push him the rest of the way.

Get Up as Soon as You Can

If you have the opportunity to get up, take it. Sometimes a fighter will stay on the ground simply because he doesn't think about getting up. If you have the option to get up, do so quickly. Use your control holds or precision strikes to make the transition.

Use Your Verbal Commands

In the heat of a fight, it's not always apparent to the suspect what you want him to do. Tell him loudly and clearly that you want him to stop fighting, to stop resisting, to turn over, to lie still, and so on. This also creates witnesses who will understand what you are doing and therefore will be more likely to testify in your behalf.

There are martial artists and police officers who like fighting on the ground. I'm not one of them. Whenever I have taken a suspect down and used constraint holds to get him controlled and handcuffed, I have always ended up with abrasions on my knuckles, knees, and elbows from the cement or asphalt. I hate that.

For sure there are powerful techniques that can be applied while on the ground, even when you are on your back. Nonetheless, there is great risk when you are down there, especially the risk of losing your gun. Many officers have told me of fighting suspects on the ground and having their weapon fall out of their holsters. One friend of mine fought a suspect in the backseat of his patrol car for several minutes, eventually getting him handcuffed (I didn't ask him why the suspect was back there without cuffs). My friend then drove the suspect to jail, and when he opened the car door, he found his service revolver lying on the seat next to the suspect. It was nighttime, and neither the suspect nor my friend had noticed that the gun had fallen out of the holster during the struggle.

Do your best to stay on your feet.

Chapter 6

How to Create a Witness

Most, if not all, officers with a few years in the trenches can relate stories of so-called witnesses who claim and complain that they saw the big nasty police officer attack a poor citizen for "no reason at all."

That's true, sir. Officers are in the habit of, without provocation, jumping innocent citizens and thumping the crap out of them, slamming on the handcuffs, throwing them headfirst into the back of a police car, and then zipping them off to jail—all for "no reason at all."

Wouldn't you just love to slap the next idiot who makes that stupid accusation? At least he couldn't say he got slapped for no reason at all.

As frustrated as we get at what onlookers claim to have seen, we have to keep in mind that people are always going to be, well, people. They perceive things based on a combination of what they see, what they think they see, what they want to see (which usually means that they want to believe the worst about the police), and what they see through a mind filter of their life experiences up to that point, including good, bad, and indifferent contacts with the police.

So, is there anything you can do about this fact of human nature to help you when you are making an arrest or are involved in some other kind of situation where onlookers are craning their necks to see what is going on? Yes, there is something, and it's based on the power of suggestion, though I call it, "create a witness." Let's look at how three of my compadres and I recently caused a scene making a routine arrest, and then look at how we could have done it more positively.

THE DOPE DEAL

My partner and I just happened to be passing by a busy street corner where an undercover police drug-buy was going down. One of the officers radioed a description of a female he wanted stopped because she had just sold him cocaine. A half minute later we saw the woman scurrying along the crowded sidewalk, and a second later, we saw two uniformed officers on bicycles jump the curb and roll right up on either side of her. But she was too quick for them; before they could dismount from their Schwinn steeds, she tossed something into her mouth.

By the time we stopped and scrambled out of our car, the bike officers were struggling with the woman to keep her from swallowing the balloons of coke (drugs are often packaged in balloons about the size of the tip of your little finger). One officer held her by the arms while the other had his hand clamped on her jaw to prevent her from swallowing the evidence. I pulled out my handcuffs, and my partner grabbed her legs since she was kicking like a crazed mule. This tussle went on for about 30 seconds while a crowd of finely dressed shoppers shouted the ol' police brutality slogan at us.

Our efforts were in vain, because the little doper swallowed the balloons, sending the evidence to where the sun never shines. A bike officer helped me get the cuffs on her, and then we half-walked, half-carried the squirming twit across the sidewalk to the car. But before we could place her in the backseat, an uptown society woman (just like the type the Three Stooges always messed with in their movies) barged out of the crowd and huffed with indignation, "Why I have never . . ."

I was about to reply in my best Groucho Marx voice, "Well, I can see why you have never," but the society matron finished her sentence.

". . . seen such police brutality. Four of you assaulting this little lady. Why you should be ashamed . . ."

I was in no mood for this woman's barrage, especially since the doper had chomped into her own tongue and spit blood on my arm.

"Here, lady," I said, thrusting the little bleeder at arm's length toward the full-bodied woman with the mink coat and Easter hat. "You stick your hand in her mouth and get the cocaine for us. You see, without it we don't have a case, and if any of the balloons break open in her stomach she will probably die."

The woman's look of pious outrage abruptly changed to one of sudden enlightenment, like, hmm, maybe the police do know what they are doing. She then did an about-face and hurried off to her nice, safe luncheon.

Although the woman was the only person to step forward, others in the crowd were not happy. They were angry with what they perceived to be wrongful conduct by the police—four officers beating up one little girl. If they later testified in court, or if they were to file a complaint with the mayor's office, the chief, or internal investigations, that is exactly what they would say.

Could we have handled this routine arrest differently? Definitely. While we probably couldn't change the way it went down, we could have done and said a few subtle things that would have helped people see what we were really doing. By doing so, we would have created good witnesses—people to support us and testify in our favor.

For example, while we struggled with the woman, one or all of us should have made statements loud enough to not only give direction to the suspect, but to "color in" what the onlookers were seeing. Statements such as the following:

"You are under arrest!"
"Stop resisting!"
"Don't swallow the cocaine!"
"Stop fighting us!"

By saying "you are under arrest" loud enough for the crowd to hear, we would have indirectly informed them that we were conducting police business and that the female we were struggling with had broken the law. The words "stop resisting" would have implanted in the minds of the onlookers that the woman was resisting to prevent us from arresting her, and the force they saw us use was necessary to counter her force. "Don't swallow the cocaine" would have informed them that this was a drug situation involving this woman and the police. And the words "stop fighting us" would convey that we didn't want to use force and that we wanted her to stop fighting. By using these phrases, we would have informed the crowd that they were witnessing a drug suspect resisting the police.

Although there are usually some witnesses who are in a position to see a police situation unfold from its beginning, some are not. Most often, the people who complain about perceived police misconduct are those who come upon the situation after it has been going on for a few seconds or a few minutes. These are the nitwits who make accusations like, "No, I didn't see the poor man do anything. The police were just ganging up on him."

With these simple create-a-witness sentences, we would have conveyed to those people who saw our arrest from the beginning, and to those who walked up while we were in the middle of it, that we were just doing our job and it was the suspect who was making it difficult for us.

WHEN YOU STILL GET A COMPLAINT

Would we have convinced everyone? Of course not. I can tell

you from experience, however, that we would have made an impression on many of them. If one of them did complain, the investigator could ask, "Did you hear the officers give the suspect any orders?"

Unless the complainant is a liar and just out to try to get the police in trouble, he would have to answer, "Uh, yeah. I heard them tell her several times to stop resisting."

"And did she?"

"Well, uh, no."

"Did the police tell her she was under arrest, and did they say anything about narcotics?"

"Uh, yeah. I heard them say that several times."

"But she kept resisting?"

"Yes."

"So the officers were trying to arrest her for narcotics—you heard them say that, right?"

"Well . . . uh . . ."

"But she kept resisting arrest?"

"Yeah, I guess so."

"So, what is your complaint again?"

Sure, it won't always be this cut-and-dried, but I guarantee that when you create a witness, you will save yourself many complaints in the end. I know of situations where officers got one or two complaints about using excessive force during an arrest, but also received five commendations for the same situation. It's all about perception. With your help, your verbalization, your painting a picture for onlookers, you will create witnesses who will support your actions.

A VARIATION

Another create-a-witness technique is to go to the onlookers after the situation is over and tell them what happened. I know one martial artist police officer who has been in several resist-arrest situations where he uses his Filipino fighting techniques to get control of a resisting suspect and ultimately the situation. Once the suspect is placed in the backseat of the police car, the officer always walks over to the onlookers, apologizes that the situation had to happen in their presence and in their neighborhood, and explains what the suspect has done to warrant the force used against him. My friend says this always works like a charm and always results in witness support when the case goes to court. He has even received written commendations from the people he has taken the time to talk to.

Of course, you are not going to convince onlookers that you are the best thing since the invention of peanut butter if they just saw you take all of your stress and aggressions out on some poor slob who only swiped a can of soup from the supermarket and stiffened his arm when you grabbed him. Create-a-witness techniques are used to color in what people are seeing. Since onlookers rarely know the whole situation when they see the police in action, create-a-witness provides them with tidbits of information that change their perception.

OTHER SITUATIONS

You stop a car being driven by a holdup suspect, and he scrambles out the driver's door.

"Police!"

"We know you are armed!"

"Keep your hands away from your body!"

"Do exactly as we tell you or you will be shot!"

After the gun smoke clears and witnesses are interviewed, they will be asked questions like these.

- "Did the police identify themselves?"
- "Did they tell the suspect to keep his hands away from his body?"
- "Did they tell him to obey their commands?"
- "Did the suspect jerk his hand toward his waistband?"
- "How many shots did you hear before the suspect fell?"

Consider the unwanted drunk in the bar:

"Come along sir."

"Now, now, don't resist us."

"Don't jerk your arm around."

"Walk nicely now and don't fight us."

Later the witnesses will be interviewed and asked the following questions:

- "Were the officers polite?"
- "Did they tell the man not to resist, not to fight?"
- "Did he continue to flail his arms around even though the officers were trying to walk him out of the bar?"
- "The officers used force, but was it after they told him to stop resisting?"

OK, you get the idea. You can probably come up with a hundred scenarios where you can use create-a-witness. There is nothing tricky or unethical about it. Your create-a-witness techniques counter how human nature and the often inaccurate elements of perception taint onlookers. You are simply providing them with reality-based suggestions that open their eyes to see what is really happening.

Point of interest: The little doper in my war story turned out to be the wrong suspect. She fit the description the undercover officer put out on the radio, but she wasn't the one who had just sold him cocaine. Nonetheless, she had cocaine in her possession, and although she swallowed a couple of balloons full of it when she saw the bike officers, she had more in her pocket. So we popped her for that.

Small world.

Chapter

7

Dream List

It's only a dream . . . only a dream . . . only a . . .
There will be a heavy snowfall in Hell before any of the things listed below will happen. But we can dream, can't we?

UNLIMITED TRAINING TIME IN THE ACADEMY

Wouldn't it be nice if the administration in your agency said this: "You've got all the time you need to turn the recruits into experts at defensive tactics. We'll cut the time for cultural-diversity training in half; we'll reduce the time for the ethics class; we'll reduce the fuzzy, feel-good training in community policing; and we'll eliminate the three hours scheduled for the 'How to Fold Your Raincoat' class. Take all the time you need for defensive tactics and do what you've got to do to ensure that those officers know how to take care of themselves so they will always finish their shift in one piece."

Never happen, you say? You're right. But remember that this is only a dream. The dream continues . . .

An Hour and a Half of Defensive Tactics
Each Day in the Academy

Our recruits get 16 weeks of academy. At five days a week, that's 80 days of training. Multiply that by one and a half hours of defensive tactics each day and you have 120 hours. That's the equivalent of six months of martial arts training for a student who goes to a private martial arts school twice a week. Can you imagine how good you would be at defensive tactics after that much training?

Fitness Training and Defensive Tactics
Should Not Be Blended

Some academies allow for 12 hours of defensive tactics and then include a mile run as part of the class. Even if the recruits can run a mile in eight minutes, by the time they prepare to run and then cool down, at least 20 minutes are gone, leaving 40 minutes for defensive tactics. So, if you are only getting 40 minutes during each of the one-hour classes, quick math shows that you are really getting only a little over five hours of defensive tactics training in your entire course. This is ridiculous. Your time would be better spent skipping stones across a lake.

Defensive tactics training should be just that: defensive tactics. No jogging, no push-ups, no stupid side-straddle hops. Yes, you should do a little warm-up, especially the knees, the wrists, and the elbows, but then get on to the training.

INSTRUCTORS WITH
EXTENSIVE BACKGROUNDS IN GRAPPLING

We want instructors who know all the answers. If they don't know the answers, they won't bullshit their way out of it, but will quickly find the answer and get back to us.

I learned early that you can bullshit recruits, but you can't do it to the regulars. If you do and they catch you at it, it will take a long time to get your credibility back, if ever. Instructors should learn all they can about the subject. When a question arises that stumps them, they should admit that they don't know, then find out the answer and get back to the class with it. If by not knowing the instructor loses a little credibility, he will quickly regain it when he returns with the answer. In addition, he should not overexplain or try to justify why he doesn't know the answer. He should say something like, "Hey, good question. I've never been asked that before, and I don't think I really have the best answer for you. Let me look into it, and I'll get back to you next time." The instructor will not only retain his credibility, but he will learn something new, too.

The greater the experience the trainers have in police work and in the martial arts, the more thorough the training, and the less likely there will be unanswered questions.

ONGOING TRAINING

This was discussed earlier, but it definitely deserves a spot on the "dream list." Here is a little question I'd like to pose to the police administrations around the country: HOW IN THE HELL DO YOU EXPECT OFFICERS TO RETAIN THEIR TRAINING IF THEY NEVER RETURN TO IT AFTER THE BASIC ACADEMY?

Sorry, I didn't mean to shout, but I find it so absurd that officers in some agencies never get refresher training of any kind or additional defensive tactics after their initial training. Inevitably, three or four years after the academy, an officer is held liable for injuries he caused while fighting with a resisting suspect. A worst-case scenario is when an officer gets hurt in a fight.

I think more officers should sue their agencies for insufficient training in defensive tactics, especially when it can be shown statistically how many physical confrontations officers get into across the country. How many of the thousands of injuries received each year by officers making physical arrests could have been avoided if they had been better trained in defensive tactics?

In my dream, officers receive ongoing training in defensive tactics. Once a week would be nice, twice would be better.

ENTHUSIASTIC STUDENTS

There is nothing more discouraging to an instructor than to have students who don't want to be in class. You usually don't find this attitude in the basic recruit academy, although there are always the know-it-alls who think that because they have big biceps or because they had a year of experience on a university police department that they already have all the answers.

I was teaching a reserve class once in which there was a guy from England who had been a bobby there for a couple of years. Just before I made my opening remarks to the class, he walked up to me, introduced himself as an ex-bobby, and told me he would help teach "these kids." He then stood beside me and faced the class as if he were my teaching partner. Well, it took me 14, maybe 15, seconds to make it clear to him who was the teacher and how he was going to get out of my space and join the others. As it turned out, he was one of the worst students in the class.

Reluctant students are often found at in-service training, where veteran officers spend up to a week getting refresher training and introduced to new material. Not all are reluctant, but there are always a few who feel they already have all the answers, so anything new is just "new-age bullshit."

I frequently teach for private security organizations, where there are always a few students who are dead-set against the training. I've even had some classes where the supervisors were angry about having to be there, having been forced to attend by upper management to satisfy a legal requirement. I once taught a class of eight mental health workers, where only two of them would get off their fat butts and try my techniques. The others argued that they could handle any situation with their psychology. That class was a long three hours to teach, and when they called me six months later for refresher training, I asked, "Refresh what?" and turned down the $200 job.

In my dream I see a class full of hungry students hanging on to my every word, and because they are so desperate for knowledge, they practice continually, through their 10-minute breaks, through their lunch hour, and even stay after class to practice more. As a result, their techniques are flawless, their confidence is high, and they can apply what they learn out in the mean, cold, concrete jungle.

Sadly, this is all just a dream.

Chapter

8

Bullets

Here are a several fortune-cookie-like tidbits of information that are worth your mulling over. They are as meaty in what they convey as they are simplistic in their form. Read them, think about them, and keep them in mind when you are discussing defensive tactics with other students and instructors.

- No magic bullet exists that will control every subject in every situation.
- No device or physical technique guarantees 100 percent success in a fight.
- You should be flexible in your response to a confrontation.
- Some mentally disturbed people may not be affected by chemical sprays.
- Some mentally disturbed people may become more combative when sprayed.

- Pain compliance holds don't always work on people under the influence of alcohol or drugs.
- Don't forsake time-proven techniques just because someone said something negative about them.
- The element of surprise plays a crucial role in a fight.
- Realistic training is more important than the newest gadget or trick hold.
- Officers rarely train for a surprise assault.
- Before you rush into a dangerous situation unnecessarily, think about your kids.
- It is your responsibility to win in a fight.
- Never threaten a suspect.
- If a situation calls for you to hit a suspect, hit him until he is no longer a threat or he gives up.
- Never agree to mutual combat.
- When writing your reports, describe in detail the force you used.
- If you threaten first, you take away the element of surprise.
- Train so that when you are in a real situation, you can say, "Been there, done that."
- Sweat in your training so you will never bleed in the street.
- Handcuffs are minimum control only.
- Be aware of your rearview mirror when you are driving home. The suspect you arrested may have gotten out before you finished writing your reports and is now following you.
- Never relax in the presence of your prisoner.
- When confronted by two attackers, avoid forming a triangle. Try to get one in front of the other.
- Keep relatives and friends away from your prisoner.
- Never underestimate anyone.
- Remember, there is always a chance you could lose your gun.
- If someone tries to take away your gun, gouge his eyes, punch his throat, do whatever it takes to keep it.
- You establish a psychological advantage when you dump the suspect onto the ground.
- When an opportunity presents itself in a fight, take advantage of it. Opportunities are like bubbles rising to the sur-

face of a lake: they appear, they pop, and then they are gone forever.

- A person who resists your come-along hold should be dealt with quickly.
- Handcuff every prisoner.
- Most suspects attack officers with their hands.
- In a survival situation, a suspect who can't see or can't stand up ain't worth much.
- When a suspect takes you down to the ground, try to land on top of him with your knees.
- When fighting for your life, the suspect becomes your enemy.
- Never underestimate a small suspect.
- Learn carotid constraint even if your agency doesn't teach it. It may save your life.
- Call for medical assistance if there is any question as to the suspect's condition after applying carotid constraint.
- Not everyone can be rendered unconscious with carotid restraint control techniques.
- Learn the basics, then apply them to your personal style.
- Never say, "That would never happen in a fight."
- Never handcuff a prisoner's hands in front of him.
- Maintain a control hold even after you have handcuffed your suspect.
- Remember that nerve-point control doesn't work on everyone.
- A vicious dog can be choked out with a forearm across his neck.
- To temporarily blind a suspect, strike him in the nose.
- Never hit a suspect with your gun.
- When you are hurt in a fight, eat the pain and continue.
- Avoid hitting a suspect with your fist; use your palm.
- If the situation permits, explain to onlookers what they just witnessed.
- Avoid touching people unless you are going to arrest them.
- If you are male, don't let a sneering crowd influence how thoroughly you search a female.
- Create-a-witness techniques might save you much stress later.
- Visualization techniques are easy, and you don't have to take a shower after working out.

- Always detail your use-of-force techniques in your reports so that you are never accused of hiding something.
- Be leery when a suspect exhibits the German shepherd stare.
- Use the high/low principle.
- If you have to hit, hit hard.
- Control your emotions.
- Know in your mind that you could beat a suspect to death if it is the only option.
- Don't let the suspect's race, sex, or ethnicity determine the degree of force used.
- Female gang members are often used to carry the gang's weapons.
- Respect begets respect.

TRAIN HARD AND BE SAFE.

About the Author

Loren W. Christensen has been studying the martial arts since 1965. Over the years he has earned 10 black belts, seven in karate, two in jujitsu, and one in arnis.

As a karate competitor, he won more than 50 trophies in the black belt division. His many articles have appeared in all martial arts magazines, and he is featured in the book *Who's Who in the American Teacher's Association of the Martial Arts*.

Loren's experience in law enforcement began in 1967 when he served in the army as a military policeman in the United States and in Vietnam. He joined the Portland, Oregon, Police Bureau in 1972, and, while still a rookie on probation, he began teaching defensive tactics to officers hired only a few months after him. Over the years, he worked the training unit, gang unit, dignitary protection, and all the precincts as a street officer.

During his career, Loren has trained hundreds of police officers in the Portland Police Bureau and in many other law enforcement agencies. He has also taught private security organizations, transient system authorities, liquor control investigators, and several other organizations.

Two weeks before completing this book, Loren retired from the police bureau after working in law enforcement for 29 years.

Today, he teaches his blend of karate, jujitsu, and arnis to a small group of private students and consults and advises a variety of businesses on the subject of security and self-defense.